The Gift of Hurt

by

Pamela Crabtree

Copyright © 2001 by Pamela Crabtree
All rights reserved.
No part of this book may be reproduced, restored in a retrieval system, or transmitted by means, electronic, mechanical, photocopying, recording, or otherwise, without written consent from the author.

ISBN: 0-75962-760-6

This book is printed on acid free paper.

1stBooks - rev. 5/24/01

I dedicate my book lovingly to my husband, Fred, my children, my grandsons, and my extended family.

Table of Contents

Part I
- Chapter One .... The Kidnapping 3
- Chapter Two .... The Horror Continues 6
- Chapter Three .... A Weekend With Oprah 21

Part II
- Chapter Four .... Little Ellie 27
- Chapter Five .... A Visit With The Dead 38
- Chapter Six .... A Good Friend 40
- Chapter Seven .... The Fall Begins 44
- Chapter Eight .... Mom, Dad, And Grandma, Too 54
- Chapter Nine .... The Fall Continues 56
- Chapter Ten .... The Steel Persona 60
- Chapter Eleven .... The Deadly Revelation 62
- Chapter Twelve .... An Almost Deadly Turn Of Fate 71

Part III
- Chapter Thirteen .... Beloved Nemesis 75
- Chapter Fourteen .... A Sickening Disclosure 81
- Chapter Fifteen .... My Friend The Shotgun 83
- Chapter Sixteen .... Goodbye Ann 87
- Chapter Seventeen .... The Reunion 90
- Chapter Eighteen .... Rejection Personified 93
- Chapter Nineteen .... Digging An Even Deeper Hole 96
- Chapter Twenty .... The Graduation 98
- Chapter Twenty-One .... Come And Get Me 101
- Chapter Twenty-Two .... Dr. Smith, Please Help Me 103
- Chapter Twenty-Three .... The Madness Escalates 106
- Chapter Twenty-Four .... The Long Walk Into Oblivion 110
- Chapter Twenty-Five .... The Controversial Dr. Smith 113
- Chapter Twenty-Six .... The End Commences 115
- Chapter Twenty-Seven .... A Talent Discovered 118
- Chapter Twenty-Eight .... An Almost Deadly Revelation 122
- Chapter Twenty-Nine .... Déjà-Vu 126
- Chapter Thirty .... The Awakening 127
- Chapter Thirty-One .... Epilogue 132

Introduction

As you begin reading my book I have several ambitious hopes for you. First, that you will allow yourself to experience my life-altering situations rather than condemning them. Secondly, that you will look at this book as my catharsis rather than another family expose'. Thirdly, that you'll try to understand, even analyze my actions. And lastly, that you'll see how I have changed-blossomed, if you will, because of the obstacles I have vaulted, although at times I have become impaled by those same obstacles.

I relate those experiences to you not so much because they are unique in and of themselves in the cycle of life, but because I have struggled through and conquered more than my share of life's tragedies and traumas.

All the individuals mentioned in this book are real, although I have changed their names. I have not exaggerated the truth for the truth needs no puffing up. You may feel surprise, confusion, disgust, disappointment and even anger while reading this book. You may see yourself or a loved one mirrored in my pain of humanness and destruction. You will be allowed into my mind through many of my personal writings and you will live through my valleys of volatile madness and its peaks of rationality and acute awareness.

The Gift of Hurt was written through my eyes which have been tainted with violations, disappointments, perversions, sex, hate, prejudice, anger, violence and jealousy. Those same eyes have been tempered with love, support, patience, tenacity, resiliency and sacrifice. All the above, the good and the evil have lead me to unprecedented fulfillment and accomplishment in spite of devastating adversity. I would like my book to be considered a major tool in identifying the epitome of living, which is the joy of loving, connecting and developing emotional intimacy with people.

It has not been easy for me to reveal family indiscretions and foibles for each life truly contains its personalized good and evil, its temperers and taints. It has been painful, at best, for me to relive these moments especially reflecting on my affection for my two psychotherapists. Nevertheless, it was a necessity if I was to write a true account of my life's experiences. In reality, Ellie Jameson, victim and mental invalid, no longer exists. What has been resurrected is Ellie Jameson, survivor, who has learned to live happily with the gift of hurt.

PART I

Pamela Crabtree

Chapter One

THE KIDNAPPING

"Get in the trunk or I'll blow your fucking head off. I'm a junkie and I don't care who sees it," threatened the customer-turned-kidnapper as he pushed the silver barrel of his revolver under the pale chin of the forty-six-year-old car salesman. The portly, blond salesman did as he was told and slowly climbed into the trunk of the car. He was ordered to give the abductor his wallet, watch, and rings.

The kidnapped victim was my husband, Matt. He reluctantly gave the kidnapper his silver wedding band of twenty-five years, his Timex watch, his college class ring, and his wallet, which had belonged to his father. Just as he tried to rise and ask the man a question, the lid slammed shut on his head, knocking him unconscious. When he awoke, he felt the car in motion and breathed the fumes from the exhaust, which was just a hand's reach beneath him. He had no idea how long he had been unconscious because the darkness inside the suffocating metal tomb kept him in blindness.

Sickened by the fumes and thinking that his bruised head could not possibly ache more, he was jolted by the blaring of rap music. The density of the bass on the music was both deafening and made his heart beat so fast he thought it would explode. In a panic he screamed for help. No one responded. He screamed again. The car came to a sudden stop, smashing him against the luxurious interior of his death box.

He heard the door open and slam shut and then an angry pounding on the trunk. A voice shouted through the metal trunk, threatening to kill him if he made any more noise. Frightened, he obeyed his captor. He heard the retreating steps and then the opening and closing of the car door. Shortly, the car began to move again.

The next few hours put the car in a stop and go mode. Matt seemed less frightened when the car was in motion, looking at it as a stay of execution. It was the stops that terrified him—awaiting the kidnapper's next move.

At one stop there was arguing—"You motherfucker, give me the money,"—then the sound of gunshots. He closed his eyes, took a deep breath, and waited to die. He heard a woman's voice scream, "Calm down, I'll get ya the money."

A few minutes later the car was in motion, and the vulgar rap music began to blare again.

As time went on, Matt's courage returned. He tried signaling for help by pushing part of his white handkerchief out the crevice of the trunk. While he held onto the end, he hoped that the other side of the waving hanky would attract attention. He prayed out loud, "God, oh God, please let someone see it." Someone did see it. The problem was that it was the kidnapper. When he heard the key slip in the trunk lock, Matt braced himself for death. The lid opened about a foot and the kidnapper shouted, "If you try that again, I'll shoot right through the trunk and kill you, you fucker."

Matt fell back in relief and passed out again. When he awoke, he tried to stretch out of his forced fetal position, but he did not have the room to do it. With tears streaming down his pale cheeks, he fondly remembered the weekend before when he walked his only daughter down the aisle and reluctantly gave her hand to Bob Randall.

It was a grand day, the culmination of months of preparation. It was Sweetest Day, in the early 1990s. Our daughter, Beth, made a beautiful bride. She was about to marry Bob, not our first choice for a husband, but we were nevertheless adjusting to the fact that he was joining our family. We had our qualms about him because he had dissolved a relationship with a woman a few years older than he in which he had fathered three sons. We never kept our feelings regarding his children hidden from Bob, and in spite of the tension, Bob said he understood us. He reiterated that he loved Beth and really felt they could make a go of it. We hesitantly accepted him, but still maintained a wait-and-see attitude. In reality, we could have ranted and raved and forbid Beth to marry Bob, but that would have accomplished absolutely nothing. Beth was a strong-willed child and an even stronger-willed woman who was deeply in love.

The blue-skied, sunny day started off with a limousine ride to my mother-in-law's house where she joined us on the ride to the church. It was my idea to pick her up and make her an important part of this special day. I always made a concerted effort to include my mother-in-law in as much of our family doings as possible. She was a very difficult person, not because she slung insults and demanded her way, but because she seemed disinterested in anything we did. To say she had a passive personality would be an understatement. She had her moments of passion, however, like when my father-in-law died in her arms from a heart attack, or later when Matt was kidnapped. Most of the time she was just there—never contributing to the conversation, offering apologies and taking blame when none was necessary.

One example was the time she found out Beth and I were in an argument. She said, "I'm sorry, was it my fault?" Her comments made me angrier with her than Beth. She knew very well that it was not her fault and that Beth and I have our moments when we spout off nasty and cruel things to one another—nobody's fault—it's just the way we are. In a few days it blows over, and we are talking again. There is no mother/daughter more devoted and loving than Beth and me.

The wedding ceremony went off without a hitch. As a gift to Bob, right after they spoke their vows, Beth, in her beautiful voice, sang "Perhaps Love" while staring into Bob's teary blue eyes. He was touched at this unique surprise included in the ceremony. Afterward, the newlyweds and the wedding party spent the afternoon driving around in the limo and drinking champagne. They arrived at the reception at 6 p.m., and after the introduction of the wedding party by the DJ the festivities began.

It was a fun reception. Everyone had a grand time eating, drinking, dancing, and socializing. We spared no expense, although we were hardly in a position to put on an extravagant wedding. We only had one daughter and wanted that day to be a special one as she started her new life.

Bob and Beth spent their wedding night at a local hotel, while the rest of us went home. It was about two in the morning, and I was still wound up and could not get to sleep when the phone rang. It was Beth. They had made love and Bob fell asleep; she just wanted to talk with me.

"I'm so happy. It was a great wedding and a great wedding night. Thanks for a great day, Mom, we'll stop over before we leave on our honeymoon and open our gifts."

The day after the wedding, we invited a few guests over to join Bob and Beth as they opened their gifts. Leftover food from the reception was served, and a short time later the newlyweds left for Niagara Falls.

While on their honeymoon Beth called me each evening and gave me an update on what they had been doing and seeing. Five days into their honeymoon, Matt was kidnapped.

"God, help me, what do I say when she calls to give me a happy update on her honeymoon excursions?"

I had to decide what to tell her. Should I wait until the body of her murdered father was found, or simply tell her that her father had been kidnapped and we didn't know what would happen. I could offer to keep her posted, but ruining her honeymoon at that moment served no purpose. If her knowledge of the kidnapping would help her father, I would tell her in a minute. I made the decision to play the role, when she called, by conducting the biggest cover-up of my life. I also decided that in the morning, if her father's body was found, I would call her hotel and ask her to come home. But until his body was discovered I would not tell her anything. That Thursday was the only evening during her honeymoon that she never called. Later, after she returned home and found out about Matt, she told me that on that particular evening they were so busy and she was so tired when they returned to their room that she did not feel like calling.

Chapter Two
THE HORROR CONTINUES

Thank God I never had to make that dreaded phone call. When they returned from their honeymoon, Matt and I took turns telling Beth and Bob about the kidnapping. We started by focusing on the 33-year-old abductor and his police blotter, which could shame the most sadistic criminal and easily wallpaper an entire room.

Having eaten most of his meals behind bars, the habitual lawbreaker compromised his freedom by his torturous attack on Matt.

Matt began his story by telling Beth and her new husband about his introduction to Hartman, which started off innocuously enough when Hartman entered the primo dealership to test-drive a red luxury car.

I interjected that earlier in the day I had met Matt at Grandma's house, where we ate bologna sandwiches and potato chips. I admitted that after exchanging angry words, we bid one another and Grandma a tension-filled goodbye. Matt resumed telling the story and said that he headed back to the dealership while I returned to my job as a secretary at a local university. There was a pause while Beth and Bob read about the entire ordeal as featured in the local newspaper and viewed videotapes about the kidnapping that appeared on local TV. During that pause, Matt sat in his brown recliner, staring straight ahead, and I sat in my favorite chair and remembered how Matt came to sell cars.

When Matt secured the position at Williams New Cars, I was less than pleased, even embarrassed, with his new job as a car salesman. I thought car salesmen were almost the lowest forms of life, with only insurance salesmen lower. However, there was money to be made for a real dealer in that industry and I had hoped that maybe after living through a roller-coaster career in transportation as a dispatcher and terminal manager, Matt might be able to make some significant money in his new occupation. It had been a rough road careerwise for him, and we had every hope that this position would be the magical job for him. Although he enjoyed the challenge of selling, he despised the owner. He felt the man treated Matt and the other salesmen like servants and must have believed, like me, that car salesmen were pretty much the lowest life form on earth. Matt once told me that the owner, Harry, called him stupid because he did not know the answer to a question.

Returning from his zombie-like stare, Matt continued telling Beth and Bob about the kidnapping. He said that after trying to sooth his frazzled ego and salvage his afternoon, after our angry exchange at lunch, he became hopeful when a customer came in requesting to test-drive a new car. Adhering to the policy that Harry imposed on the salesmen—that they must go out on all test-drives with customers—Matt grabbed the keys to the car. Though he was reluctant to get in the car with the leather-jacketed black man, he had every hope that this could be the sale of the day. He learned early on that looks and attire made no difference as to who bought a new car. He had sold cars to men who dressed poorly but had the cash to pay the $30,000-plus for a car.

After giving the young black man the keys to the car, Matt took the seat next to him. As they were driving, Matt explained all the amenities of the car to the man, who said his name was Willie Hartman.

"You'll notice the real leather interior and automatic temperature control."

"Yeah, I see that, but I want to look in the trunk."

Hartman turned into an alley and stopped the car. Matt kept talking while he cautiously got out of the car, then immediately became suspicious and looked around for other men he thought were waiting to jump him. He looked around as he headed toward the back of the car. After Hartman popped the trunk, he pulled a silver-barreled revolver out of his jacket and ordered Matt to get into the trunk or, "I'll blow your fucking head off. I'm a junkie and I don't care who sees me."

Matt climbed in and watched terrifyingly as the trunk lid slammed shut. Hartman got back in the car and drove off into what was to become the most terrifying, traumatic experience of Matt's life.

Minutes, which seemed like hours, passed and the car finally stopped. Matt, in a panic, started to pound uncontrollably on the trunk lid.

"Help, get me out of here."

Hartman opened the trunk a few inches, "Keep your fucking mouth shut or I'll shoot through the trunk and shut you up permanently."

Fearful of being shot, he quieted down.

While the kidnapping was actually happening, I was just finishing up my duties at work, and because Matt always worked late on Thursdays and would not be home until 9:30, I decided to do the grocery shopping for the week. After the grocery store, I headed straight home. Just as I pulled into the driveway a little after seven, my youngest sons, Thomas and Rick confronted me and excitedly said, "The sheriff called and wants you to call right away."

Of course I dropped everything and called back with terror in my heart. The deputy asked, "Do you know where your husband is?"

"Yes, he's at work."

"No, he left this afternoon with a new car."

"My husband would never steal a car."

"That's not what I mean, please call your husband's employer."

I hung up the phone and immediately called the dealership.

Henry, Matt's boss, told me sadly, "Matt has been missing since this afternoon. A man called about three p.m. and said that he spotted the car with a black man driving, but there was no sign of Matt. Ellie, they're calling it foul play."

I remember feeling a numbness engulf my body. A sense of confusion also followed as I tried to comprehend that this heinous crime had happened to Matt.

I did not cry. I moaned and ran outside with the cordless phone still in my hand. I cried out for Randy, my oldest son, to come home. He was standing in front of his girlfriend's house across the street. He came running and as he approached, I screamed, "Your father's been kidnapped."

I continued telling the newlyweds that Randy and I hugged and retreated inside the house. I knew that Grandma must be told. But I could not do it—I did not know how to tell her. I called Aunt Linny and told her what had happened and asked her to please tell Grandma. From all accounts, told to me later, Aunt Linny called Aunt Hilley, and the two of them drove to Grandma's house to tell her of the kidnapping.

I called Aunt Julie and then Uncle Ken and Uncle Paul, who were bowling, and in a span of an hour our house filled up with relatives and concerned neighbors. I called one of my supervisors and told her what happened. She tried to comfort me by telling me that, "Matt will be found safe."

"No, I'm sure he's been murdered."

A few minutes later I received a call from another one of my supervisors. He said he called a friend of his who was an FBI agent, and the agent told him to tell me to begin taping every phone call I received. He said Matt might have been kidnapped for a ransom. We began taping all calls. He also told me that he had contacted Captain Carlton Ray of the local police department to make sure this crime received everyone's attention.

As the newlyweds listened intensely and with tears in their eyes, I related that as the hours went on, I felt alone in the room full of people. Family members tried to comfort me, but I rejected their efforts. I did not want anyone but Matt. I walked around the house like a zombie. I prayed for news of my husband's safety. Every so often I felt a hand on my shoulder reaching out to comfort me.

A couple of hours later I walked outside. On that warm, rainy October night I saw a sheriff's car drive by. I yelled out, and she stopped. I asked if she had heard any updates on Matt's whereabouts. While I stood alongside the police car she radioed in to see if there was any new information. Just then, I heard the person on the other end of the radio say they had found the car. As my heart started pumping rapidly, they retracted their statement, saying that it was the wrong car. My head fell, again, and I went back into my cocoon of numbness.

I needed to do something—you can only wring your hands for so long. I called our bank's twenty-four-hour automated service to see if anyone had taken money out of our checking account. After entering all the confidential information I heard, "A withdrawal of $50."

"A withdrawal of $50."

"A withdrawal of $50.

A total of $150 had been taken out of our account that day. Someone, somewhere had access to Matt's money card, and I was sure that it was that man who murdered Matt.

According to the automated voice, we still had a balance of over $7,000 in our checking account. We had a large balance because the checks written to pay for Beth's wedding had not yet cleared. I called the bank's after-hours number and tried to get someone to help me. I begged, "If you could locate where the money was withdrawn then maybe we'll be able to find out the vicinity of where my husband was."

"I'm sorry we can't do anything until morning."

Livid and feeling helpless, I slammed the phone down.

Time went by very slowly. The minutes turned into hours, and by midnight I had lost any hope that Matt would be found alive. I was certain he had been murdered. I was positive that when morning came someone would discover his mutilated body in an alley or a ditch, hidden by the autumn leaves. I visualized his torture and prayed that this horrible man had killed him quickly and not left him to suffer a painful death. I pictured him being cut on his arms and legs just to make him suffer and then a knife going into his stomach. I pictured a gunshot wound to his head. Finally, I saw vivid images of him lying in a coffin. It was at that point that I decided which mortuary I would call to bury him. I picked out the suit he would be buried in—his dark blue pinstriped one—his favorite suit. I tried to figure out how to come up with the money for the funeral. I would try and get a grave at Calverton Cemetery and have his funeral mass at our home parish.

I told my brothers, Ken and Paul, "I cannot bear to identify Matt's body when it's found. The two of you must go to the morgue to identify him."

"Sis, it won't be necessary because Matt's going to be found safe."

"Please, you two identify his body, please."

"OK, OK."

After reluctantly agreeing, someone tried to comfort me, and I remember my rude response, "Leave me alone. Matt's dead and nobody is doing anything."

In retrospect, my sons needed my support, but I could not give anyone anything of myself at that time. Later I heard that Randy had taken control of the situation and was giving loving comfort to Thomas and Rick.

Seething with rage at the black man who I was sure had murdered Matt, I began to plan what to do when he went to trial. I knew that our judicial system would not satisfy my thirst for revenge, so I vowed that evening to take justice into my own hands and kill my husband's murderer. I figured I'd have to spend some time in prison, but I was sure I would get off with a light sentence under the circumstances. That revenge and hatred kept me going. It helped me keep my mind off how frightened Matt must have been just before he was shot or knifed to death.

Around midnight the house started to clear out. Randy, Thomas, and Rick retreated to a bedroom to try and get some rest. Paul stayed later than the rest, and then hugged me and left around one in the morning. I laid down on the couch in the family room and looked up and saw that the ceiling in the family room was leaking in several places from all the rain we were receiving. I thought that if we did not have bad luck, we would not have any luck at all. I placed buckets wherever there was a leak. I lay on the couch and tried to rest. I prayed for sleep, but my mind swam with thoughts of Matt's murder. I stared at the TV, not comprehending anything that was on the screen.

Around 8:30 a.m., after a couple of hours filled with an on-again, off-again twilight sleep, I decided to call the number the police had given me. The police officer answered, "Robbery/homicide."

My heart sank. I told him I was Mrs. Matt Jameson and I was checking on my husband's case. He excitedly told me, "A unit just found the car, but there is no sign of your husband, I'll call you right back."

I hung up and waited what seemed like hours, but in actuality it was only ten minutes. When the phone rang I was sure that the information on the other end of the line would be bad. I hurriedly picked up the receiver and the officer nearly shouted at me, "He's alive."

After thirteen hours of a living hell, I broke down and sobbed. The officer said, "They're transporting him to the hospital. Do you want to go to the hospital or wait until he comes home?"

"I'm going to the hospital."

"Are you okay?"

"I'm happy!"

"Drive carefully because it's wet and slippery out there."

As I started to relive the excitement and the total awe of that morning to Beth and Bob, my heart started to pound. I told them that I ran into the bedroom where Randy, Thomas, and Rick were sleeping and yelled out, "Dad's alive."

Thomas immediately sat up with a crucifix in his hand and said, "See, I told you Jesus would not let Dad die." I called Matt's mother and told her the wonderful news.

I ran out of the house and told the boys to call the family and tell them Dad had been found alive. I drove to the hospital and kept giving thanks to God and laughing, "Thank you God, oh thank you God."

I could not cry anymore, the relief felt great—I continued to laugh.

I must have driven to the hospital in record time, because the next thing I remember was driving into the emergency room parking lot. I ran into the hospital, and as I entered I shouted to the first person I saw, "I'm Matt Jameson's wife."

I found out later that that person was a doctor. He told me, "God, I love a happy ending, we have so few here," and led me to Matt's room in the trauma center. When I opened the door, I saw him lying on a bed with police officers all around him. I ran to him and jumped on top of him. We were crying, hugging, and kissing when he looked up at me and held his hands up and said, "Look, he took my rings."

"Don't worry, Babe, the important thing is that you're okay."

We reunited lovingly and with relief beyond description.

The doctor said that as soon as Matt's blood pressure was down to about normal they would release him. He was roughed up and bruised, but for the most part he was in good condition considering what he had been through. The nurse asked me to follow her so I could fill out some medical forms. I sat with her and felt a hand on my shoulder. I looked up and saw Aunt Grace standing behind me. We hugged and talked about the horrible crime. I started to sit down again to finish the paperwork when I saw Aunt Julie and Uncle Nick followed by Uncle Paul. It was a grand reunion.

I told Beth and Bob that after I finished the paperwork, we started back to Matt's room, but we met him and the detectives in the corridor. The doctor had released him with instructions that he was to visit our family doctor as soon as possible.

The detectives said they needed Matt to make a photo identification of his abductor. They said after that they would not bother him again and he could go home. They asked that we not talk to the media. We agreed, but unknown to us, reporters had already called our home and talked with Randy. Randy was quoted in the paper as saying, "It was the weirdest thing, there was a lot of crying going on in our house."

Meanwhile, Matt quickly identified the kidnapper, and we started home. When we pulled into the driveway, the boys ran out and hugged their father.

Then all hell broke loose. TV stations and the local paper all wanted interviews with Matt and me. Matt said before he talked with anyone or saw anyone he wanted to take a shower. He agreed to be interviewed in a couple of hours. Matt received telephone call after telephone call. The phone rang constantly from well wishers and people we had not heard from in years. We received a meat and cheese tray as well as lots of flowers. A couple of dear friends brought over a bottle of wine.

I found out later that one of the supervisors from my office ran down to tell Rhonda, my direct supervisor, while she was teaching class, that Matt had been found alive. They tell me she began to cry as the students cheered. Matt also received a bouquet of flowers from the employees of the car dealership. He never received a call from the owner, Harry, or Henry, the sales manager. We found out later that Harry blamed us for the adverse publicity the kidnapping caused the dealership. I told Beth and Bob that during the thirteen-hours Dad was missing, no one from the dealership called to see how we were doing or to see if we needed anything. Nevertheless, that Friday was a wonderful day and one we will always remember.

The newlyweds were in awe as I continued the kidnapping story. I reiterated that if Matt told his saga once he told it a thousand times. Each time, however, I learned something new about his ordeal. For instance, he asked Hartman, his kidnapper, to let him out so he could go to the bathroom. Hartman yelled, "Piss in your pants." After he demanded and got his rings, watch, and wallet, he told Matt that if he told anyone about the kidnapping he would kill his family. He knew where we lived because he had Matt's wallet.

Matt said that he felt helpless when he had to succumb to Hartman's demands. He said that one time he must have passed out, and when he came to he thought he was suffocating. In his panic to escape, he managed to push the trunk lid open enough to see a crack of light from the outside. He stuck his little black notebook in the crevice and could feel the cool, fresh air come into the trunk. A couple of minutes later raindrops started dripping inside the trunk. To stave off dehydration he put his hanky on his forearm and let the rain drip on it. Every so often he would suck the moisture from it.

With his survival instincts peaking, Matt managed to unhook the spare tire from the rack and position it in front of his torso. He figured that if Hartman shot into the trunk he might live if he were shot in his arms or legs. After securing the tire over his torso he felt around in the darkness until he felt the cold steel of the tire iron. He vowed that the next time Hartman opened the trunk, even a little, he would lash out and kill his kidnapper. As he recited the 23rd Psalm, he prayed to his deceased father and to God. At that moment he was resigned to dying.

Suddenly, there was a pounding on the trunk and some muffled sounds. He held the tire iron tightly in his hand waiting to strike out. The trunk opened and he heard someone shout, "He's alive." Matt's immediate response was, "Yes." Blue immediately surrounded him—the blue uniforms of the police and the paramedics. He tried to struggle out of the trunk, but the paramedics insisted he lay there until they checked his vital signs. They started an IV because he was dehydrated. While lying there with the paramedics tending to him, he saw, in the distance, Hartman being dragged away. He fought all the way to the police car.

Matt was helped out of the trunk, placed on a stretcher, and rushed to the hospital in an ambulance. He owes his life to police officer, Tom Bork, who, on a hunch that rainy Friday morning decided to go the opposite way from his normal route to look for the red car. To his surprise and relief, the hunch paid off. In the parking lot of a low-income housing complex, there it was in all its glory.

After calling for backup, Bork related that he apprehended two youths that were sitting in the back seat of the car. He pulled his gun and demanded that they take him to the person who had keys to the vehicle. They took him to Hartman, who was sleeping with the mother of one of the youths. Our credit cards were found under the mattress. Sadly, Matt's wedding band, which I placed on his finger over twenty-five-years ago, his class ring, and his father's wallet were gone, more than likely sold for drugs.

As the story about Matt concluded Beth and Bob were awestruck at all that happened while they were on their honeymoon. Beth remarked that she wished she could have been with us to offer up support.

Later in the week we read in the paper that Hartman was held on a $35,000 cash bond while his case went to the grand jury, which found cause to indict him. He was assigned a public defender and pleaded not guilty by reason of insanity. He was ordered to undergo a psychiatric evaluation.

Nothing much happened regarding Hartman's trial, and everyone affected tried to get back to normal, but we found that impossible as remnants from the kidnapping permeated our lives. Trying to keep my anger and disillusionment in check regarding the callous attitude that the car dealership adopted about the kidnapping, I phoned Harry, but was told that he was unavailable. If he had talked with me and exhibited some compassion for what Matt went through it would have helped our recovery immensely.

I had to make a decision the Saturday after the kidnapping on whether to attend a luncheon professor Janice Miller was giving in honor of Supreme Court Justice Sandra Day O'Connor. It was a great honor to be invited, and I really did not want to miss the opportunity to meet the first woman Supreme Court Justice of the United States. Matt encouraged me to attend the luncheon at a prestigious downtown club. I agreed to go when he assured me that he would be fine.

When I walked into the room at the club, Janice was standing beside Justice O'Connor. Janice came over and hugged me and asked how I was doing and how Matt was doing. She then introduced me to Justice O'Connor and explained what had happened. Justice O'Connor asked, "How is Matt doing? I read of his kidnapping in the paper."

"He is very well. Thank you Justice O'Connor for your concern."

She asked me a few more questions about Matt and the kidnapping, and then we all took our seats for the luncheon.

After the luncheon I decided that I would stop by the dealership because I wanted to find out why there was no action taken on the 3 p.m. call made the day of the kidnapping by witness Ken Fielding. After arriving at the dealership I was told, again, that Harry was out of the office. Henry inquired about Matt and then took me to the back of the garage and showed me the red car in which Matt was kept captive. Henry assured me that Matt would not be out any money, that he would be reimbursed for the $150 that was taken out of our checking account and the $250 deductible we had to pay to the insurance company to replace the jewelry.

A mechanic came up to me and asked how Matt was doing. He told me that everyone was ordered to keep quiet about the incident. The mechanic said he could not believe Harry's callousness.

Henry told Matt to take off as much time as he needed. He was off work for a week or so. It was difficult, but he managed to return to work because, "You don't make any money unless you sell cars."

When he returned to work, Harry exclaimed, "The kidnapping is over, and you are alive, so forget it." Matt tried to forget the ordeal until a customer came in the afternoon of his first day back at work and wanted to take a test drive. Matt broke down and had to leave. He never returned.

As usual, we were hard pressed for money, and the holidays were approaching. In early December Matt asked me to pick up his last commission check. He could not bear to go to the dealership himself because it triggered too many emotions. I needed to get the check into the bank as soon as possible to cover a check I wrote to the grocery store. I took my lunch hour and drove downtown to pick up the check. When I arrived at the dealership, Henry asked me to wait until Harry signed the check. I sat in a chair located directly outside Harry's office. Every so often I would lean to my left and peer into his luxurious office to see if he had completed whatever it was that kept me waiting. But he just sat in his large leather chair, in his office decorated with the finest wood furniture that contrasted beautifully with the rich natural woodworking and plush carpeting. He kept me waiting for over half an hour. After he signed Matt's check he called Henry, who then asked me to follow him to the back office. I followed like a puppy dog.

When we arrived in the back office, Henry handed the office clerk Matt's check. She mumbled something and put the check into the typewriter. She typed something on it, handed it back to Henry, and he gave it to me. I left and returned to my car and sped off to the bank. When I got to the bank I turned the check over to sign it on the back, "For deposit only." It was then that I realized what the office clerk had typed on Matt's check. It read, "PAYMENT IN FULL AND FINAL SETTLEMENT FOR ALL CLAIMS AGAINST WILLIAMS CARS NOW AND IN THE FUTURE." I broke down and sobbed. I could not deposit the check under those conditions. I returned to work and called a lawyer. The check was for $86. He did not even pay Matt minimum wage for the few hours he tried to work after the kidnapping.

Halloween and Thanksgiving in the early 1990s came and went. A week or so before Christmas, I was on my way home from work and had the local news on the radio when they reported that an inmate of the county jail had escaped—and then the kick in the stomach; the escaped prisoner was identified as Willy Hartman. I almost lost control of the car as I tried to regain my composure. I turned the volume up and listened intently. The report said that as he was being taken for his psychiatric evaluation at a mental health facility across from the jail, he managed to get away from the sheriff's deputy. The deputy's excuse for the escape was that he just turned his head for a moment, and Hartman used that opportunity to run away. When I returned home I broke the news to Matt. We cried. We were concerned because Hartman's threats to harm us could now come to fruition. We found ourselves becoming even more vigilant and feared for our safety because he knew where we lived. We decided to take extra precautions as far as securing our house. We were even afraid to let our Sheltie dog, Tillie, out alone for fear he would harm her.

Then came the good news. Not long after his escape, Hartman was apprehended. The television reported that a UPS driver was making a delivery and saw a man handcuffed and shackled running up the stairs into a church not far from the jail. He notified the police and when Hartman was returned to his prison cell he tried to commit suicide by overdosing on pills. From what the authorities told us he had stockpiled pills given to him while he was in jail. He was rushed to a local hospital and spent the night in the intensive care unit. The following day he was returned to his cell with an order from the judge that in the future Hartman would not be allowed to leave his jail cell. The psychiatric evaluation would be done in or around his cell.

Weeks passed with nothing else happening regarding his case. After the first of the year the prosecutor asked to meet with us. We were informed that our prosecutor had accepted a plea bargain from Hartman and his attorney. The agreement said that he would plead guilty to kidnapping and aggravated robbery as well as relinquish the jewelry taken in the kidnapping, and they would dismiss the escape charge and the weapons specification. The prosecutor agreed.

A date and time was set for sentencing. Meanwhile, I kept calling the prosecutor and asking if the jewelry, especially Matt's wedding band, had been recovered. He kept telling me it hadn't.

In April of the early 1990s Matt, Beth, Randy, Matt's mother, and I piled into our car and headed to the county courthouse to be there when Hartman was sentenced. We found our way to Judge Judith Lowe's courtroom and took our seats.

Hartman's attorney interrupted the prosecutor as he was talking with us and stated that Hartman had phoned a woman in the inner city and that she had Matt's wedding band. He said that he was going to send over a couple of armed police officers to retrieve it. The sentencing was delayed while the police officers tried to recover the jewelry. When the officers returned they said that the woman at the house claimed she did not know anyone by the name of Willy Hartman.

I quickly turned and stared when I saw, out of the corner of my eye, the mammoth wooden courtroom door open. In walked a procession of sheriff's deputies leading a handcuffed Hartman, who was dressed in an orange prison jumpsuit. I knew it was Hartman because his picture had been strewn all over the newspaper and TV. I squeezed Matt's hand, which I had been holding onto like a lifeline since we took our seats in the courtroom. I watched as Matt's pale face turned red with anger at the sight of his kidnapper.

Hartman never even looked at us, but we could not take our eyes off the son-of-a-bitch. I listened intently as Hartman and his attorney spoke about where the jewelry was, what street the house was located on, and what color the house was as well as saying it was a couple doors down from a church. I filed that information in the back of my head for future use. We continued to wait for the return of Matt's jewelry. The defense attorney said he was going to go to the house personally. He requested a police officer to accompany him. After receiving a short recess from Judge Lowe, they left. Unfortunately, they also returned without the jewelry. The sentencing procedure began.

Hartman was escorted to the table on the left-hand side of the courtroom facing the judge. The prosecutor took his place at a table across from Hartman, on the right. Judge Lowe entered and we were all ordered to stand. Then the bailiff told us to be seated and we heard him say, "State versus Willy Hartman." Judge Lowe asked Hartman's attorney if he had anything to say on behalf of his client. The following is the exact statement, misstatements and all, taken from the court transcripts made by Hartman's attorney.

"Yes, your honor. I know that the court knows a lot about this case since many times we've appeared in court and also there's a court diagnostic report as well as the probation report.

"We just reported to the court what happened a few moments ago. I went to a house and found a person whom Willy named who would have possession of the property of Mr. Jameson, and that person did not admit knowing my client and didn't know anything about the situation. So I came up empty there.

"I...during the course of trying to retrieve the property, I continually asked Willy if there was someone who he trusted who could do running for him. And there apparently is nobody. And I think that that's sort of remarkable in that I don't think Willy has any sort of support system in the community at all. I don't think Willy has anybody that he would trust that would be able to do these things.

"I mention that only in that I think that it's characteristic of his life. As you can see, he's been in trouble before in situations similar to this. They're serious offenses.

"Willy understands he's going to be sentenced today. He understands he's going to get time. I would ask the court to consider one thing. You have a lot of time you can hit Willy with. He understands he's going to get a big sentence. He's prepared for that today.

"I would ask that the court consider doing a somewhat different sentence in that because you have two felonies and you have big time on each one and you cap out at fifteen anyway. And I think you get—he could be up to the parole board, I think, in nine years and six months if my understanding is correct."

From that point on Mitchell tried to bargain with the judge. The judge said, "I don't believe that either of these offenses would be probatable. Since the firearm was used, I don't believe the court can do what you're asking in any event, Mr. Mitchell."

Mitchell came back with, "Okay, well in any case while the court diagnostic report did not come back and say that we met the criteria of NGRI, I think there are psychological aspects I wish the court to take into consideration. There must be a Jekyll-and-Hyde aspect to Willy. Willy has been extremely cooperative. Obviously I've not seen the part of Willy that Mr. Jameson has, and it must be very frightening. You know the escape...figures in this. There was a subsequent suicide attempt. I think there's psychological problems here. I just want the court to be aware of those when sentencing."

The judge turned to the prosecutor and asked if anyone wishes to speak. The prosecutor said, "Yes, Mr. and Mrs. Jameson."

Here is what Matt said in his victim impact statement.

"Good morning, your honor. First off, I want to thank you for giving me this time. You heard his attorney say psychological or how unbalanced that he is. I ask that you please give him the maximum sentence on every charge. Not just for my benefit for what he's done to my family, and me, but next time if you let him out he could kill somebody.

"I can't explain to you what it was like to be in that trunk all those hours and what went through my mind. And this person had no feelings for me whatsoever. He treated me like a piece of garbage. Threatened my life, even said, 'I'm a junky, I don't care, I'll kill you right here.'

"So I ask you to take that into consideration, your honor, if not just for me and my family, what they've been through, but for anybody else that he decides to do this to and possibly kill them."

The prosecutor said, "Your honor, at this time I'll read the statement by Mrs. Jameson." (I wanted to read it myself, but I broke down, and he had to read it from my paper). My statement read:

"Judge Lowe, I ask that Willy Hartman be sentenced to the maximum extent the law allows. I feel with the damage that he's done to my husband, to me, and to my children and to protect all of us from him, the fullest penalty of confinement should be given.

"Because of Willy Hartman's actions, our family will never be the same again. And that change has not been for the better. We will have the hurt, anger, distrust, and fear very likely for the rest of our lives. Since the kidnapping I live in a state of anxiety. Even though it's going on six months since the abduction, I'm still trying to cope.

"I think of the kidnapping daily. It has caused me great distress when my husband or my children go somewhere and I feel they're gone longer than they should, or if, for instance, we go out shopping. I cannot find them right away, I go into a panic.

"All sorts of things go through my mind, and it upsets me all over again. I am not the same person, nor do I feel the same about things in general. The whole incident has affected my personal and social life and my performance at work.

"I ask that Willy Hartman be sentenced to the maximum jail time, not completely as a vindictive move but as a survival tactic on my part. I am terrified that he may again stalk the streets with a weapon and hurt someone. I believe it is only a matter of time before he fatally injures one of his victims. Thank you."

The prosecutor told the judge that since 1975, when Hartman was sixteen, he had been free less than a year. Since then he had been involved in numerous juvenile violations, including aggravated robbery.

In 1979 he was sentenced to eight to thirty-five-years for aggravated robbery and kidnapping like the one Matt experienced. Then in 1986 he received three to ten years for receiving stolen property. He had an out date from the penitentiary of 2035—he had that much time hanging over his head when he committed Matt's kidnapping.

The prosecutor said, "It does not appear to me that we have any kind of candidate for rehabilitation but old age. So I therefore request the maximum sentence in this case."

The judge spoke: "At this time, Mr. Hartman, you can say anything you wish to say before sentencing is passed."

Hartman said, Your honor, I'd like to apologize to Mr. Jameson and his family for all the inconvenience I've caused them."

"I want you to turn around and say this to them if you mean it," insisted Judge Lowe.

Hartman turned to us and did indeed apologize. We all just moaned with frustration and anger because he treated the crime so lightly. He seemed so flip and nonchalant about the kidnapping.

Just before Judge Lowe passed sentence she said, "Mr. Hartman, it's much more than inconvenience we're talking about here. What concerns me are the things that the prosecutor has said about your history in this community. You don't understand what you did. You can't imagine what you did to this family. Not just to Mr. Jameson. To his wife. To his children. You picture yourself inside a trunk for eighteen hours, sir. You picture yourself not knowing if you were going to live or die. The fact that Mr. Jameson is here in the court this morning is no thanks to anything you did.

We're very lucky—you're very lucky that you're not facing an aggravated murder charge with the ultimate penalty of death because that's what could have happened here."

Something is missing in you, Mr. Hartman, because you don't understand what your actions do to others. I don't know if we call it conscience or what.

Even the reports tell me that you don't look beyond what you're feeling and what you see. You don't have any empathy for other people. There's no explanation of why you should go to a stranger and cause the terror that you caused him."

"Not only that, the few things that we were attempting to recover weren't recovered. He's lost a wedding ring, some other items that mean a lot more than just would first appear.

"You will be down in the institution, and the reason for it is that we cannot trust you in this community. We cannot trust your actions. We cannot believe that at some point you might not take a life. You were very close to doing it this time."

"For these reasons and based on your previous record and protection of the community, I order Willy Hartman committed to the care and custody of the Department of Rehabilitation and Correction on count one, aggravated robbery, for a period of no less than ten, no more than twenty-five years. As to the kidnapping charge, count two, I order him committed to the care and custody of the Department of Rehabilitation and Correction for a period of no less than ten, no more than twenty-five years. I order that the sentences be run consecutively."

We started out of the courtroom, and I remember thinking about the call I received from a representative of the Victim Assistance Program saying that someone from the program would be there to assist us and support us in court. If we needed help reading our statement to the judge they would read it. We were told that he or she would just sit with us if that were all we needed. I thought how nice it would be to have someone who knows how the system works sitting with us.

Sadly and disappointingly, we never saw anyone or received any moral support from this publicly heralded program. Thank God for the prosecutor. Although this program may be a good one for some people, we must have fallen through the cracks, as we never saw a victim assistant representative that day.

Falling through the cracks proved to be an understatement during the next few years, as we were going to discover.

The thought that someone, some low-life, had Matt's wedding band was on my mind day and night. The silver band that was blessed in a ring ceremony by our parish priest so long ago was more than just a ring. Hartman had stolen a precious and irreplaceable symbol of our love and commitment. To make matters worse, it was a Keepsake wedding band, and the jeweler said they no longer manufacture Keepsakes. I did purchase a gold wedding band for Matt, but it does not hold the sentimentality that the original held.

In my irrational quest to right a wrong, I asked a friend and co-worker, Margaret, to help me retrieve Matt's wedding band. One afternoon in April, shortly after Hartman's sentencing, Margaret and I drove to the inner-city home Hartman's attorney had described at the sentencing. I had prepared a written note practically begging for the return of the ring. I also said that a reward would be given to the person returning the ring.

Margaret suggested that she run the note up to the house and place it in the mailbox. Margaret was black and feared for my safety, me being a white woman. She went up to the house, and as she started to put the note in the mailbox a woman came out and confronted her on the front porch. Margaret gave her my note. I watched as she and the woman spoke to each other. My hopes were high that this stranger would be able to end some of our suffering. Unfortunately, the woman told Margaret that she did not know Willy Hartman. Margaret left the note with her just in case.

A week or so later I asked the local paper if they would put a note about the ring in their human interest section requesting that anyone who has knowledge of or possession of the ring to please turn it over to the prosecutor, Tim Barter, or an inner city Baptist church. It was also stated that charges would not be pressed against the person returning the ring. The Baptist church was located close to the house that the defense attorney named at Hartman's sentencing. Previously, I had talked with the minister of the church, and he willingly agreed to be the go-between. I also left the reward money with him. After a few weeks, when no one came forth, I told the minister to keep the reward money and put it into the church coffers.

Chapter Three
A WEEKEND WITH OPRAH

After the kidnapping, I was determined that we were going to get something good out of this crime. I vowed to get enough money to pay off our house and also get a free trip to New York or Chicago, for The Phil Donahue Show or The Oprah Winfrey Show. A few months after the ordeal, I wrote the Oprah Winfrey Show and told them of the kidnapping and the details. I did not receive a call from the Winfrey producers until months after my initial letter.

But when it happened, it happened quickly. One afternoon while I was at work, my son called and said that someone from the Oprah Winfrey Show called and asked that I call them back. I, of course, was thrilled and returned their call immediately. The woman asked me to relate what had happened regarding the kidnapping, and I did so. She asked to talk with Matt, which she did later, and the decision was made at Harpo Studios to ask Matt and maybe me to appear on a segment of the Oprah Winfrey Show.

Within a few days of the first call, we were flying to Chicago. Our contact person was one of Winfrey's producers, and she said that my youngest sons, Thomas and Rick, could come with us and their expenses would be paid by Harpo Productions. They also made hotel reservations for Randy and his girlfriend, Beth and Bob, and, of course, my mother-in-law. However, only our hotel and expenses were covered.

We received plane tickets by Federal Express to fly out of the local Airport into O'Hare Airport. When we landed at O'Hare, there was a limousine driver waiting for us to take us to a first-class hotel in downtown Chicago. After checking in we were each given food vouchers to cover our meals for our overnight visit. An hour or so after checking into the hotel we received a call from a representative of Winfrey's asking if our accommodations and flight were okay and saying that a limousine would pick us up at 7 a.m. and drive us to the studio for the 10 a.m. taping. They did two tapings a day, and we were to be included in the first taping.

The next morning I looked out our window around 7 a.m. and there was a black limo waiting for us. We jumped in and scooted off to the studio. When we arrived, and after entering through a secured door, we were escorted to a large room. It reminded me of a boardroom where executives meet to discuss business. It had a long, wood-grained table and comfortable chairs around it. There were coffee and donuts for us. We were the first ones there, but by taping time the room was filled with individuals who had been kidnapped or had children who had been kidnapped.

Some of the people were very nice and down to earth; however, a few of the people were pompous and self-centered. I really did not care because I was having the time of my life. They told us that we had to go to the dressing room, where they fixed our hair and dabbed some make-up on us. The assistant said that I would be in the audience, seated on the end of the row so Oprah could come over and ask me some questions if she wanted to. I would not be on stage with Matt, but I did not care. I was going to have the best of both worlds—the excitement of it all, but not the worry that I would have to be interviewed by Oprah on stage. As it turned out I was not asked anything or included in the show.

The show started by Oprah interviewing some bank employees who had been kidnapped. Sadly, one teller was killed when the kidnapper drove a car over her. Halfway through the taping, during a commercial break, they brought Matt and a man who also had been kidnapped and stuffed in the trunk of a car for seven hours on stage. They were seated next to each other. Matt told me after the show that he could have done seven hours standing on his head.

The man who was on stage with Matt just talked and talked, and even when Oprah asked Matt a question the other man would rudely butt in. He was bound and determined to not only have his fifteen minutes of fame but take Matt's fifteen minutes, too. In spite of this jerk, Matt did splendidly and maintained his composure and dignity. I was very proud of him. The only time he choked up was when Winfrey asked him how he felt in the trunk. He told her that he was worried about his family and what we must be going through. Unfortunately, the other man interrupted and told Oprah how macho he was by throwing the keys to the car at his kidnapper. It was very unappealing, and he looked quite foolish.

After the taping we were ushered back into the conference room where the day had started and were given special Oprah Winfrey mugs. We were escorted into a limousine and taken back to the hotel to rest and then prepare to fly back home. Another limousine took us to O'Hare. The show was scheduled to air a month or so later. We were excited.

In the early 1990s Matt was working at a transportation company as a dispatcher. He received a phone call one day, and the woman who transferred the call to him laughingly said, "The caller claims to be Oprah Winfrey."

"Yeah, sure it is."

The receptionist was obviously shocked and dubious about the caller. Matt was also shocked when he picked up the phone and the caller identified herself as Oprah Winfrey.

"Really, Matt, it's me, Oprah."

She proceeded to tell him that she decided not to air the show because it would give crazies a lot of ideas on how to kidnap and hurt people. She went on to say that she really appreciated Matt's help and that she would send him a tape of the show. In the future, if she would do a show on that topic she would call him. I have to admit I was very disappointed. I even thought, *All of a sudden she gets scruples on what topic to present on her show.*

When we received the tape we immediately played it, and I could see why she decided not to air it. It was not her normal format or quality. She had way too much information crammed into that hour. The whole program was disjointed and confusing. Not only that, but there were hardly any questions or interaction with the audience. And last, the man who was on with Matt was a real hot dog. He ruined what could have been an interesting, poignant story about kidnapping victims.

Now that it has all been said and done, I really would have liked Matt's story to be publicized. I had hoped someone would pick it up and try to sell the story to or a producer of a TV movie. However, after Oprah shelved the segment, all hope of notoriety ended.

One interesting footnote regarding the kidnapping came a few months after the ordeal when a woman called me and said that her sister, who lives in Germany, sent a clipping that appeared in their local German newspaper. The article was about Matt's kidnapping. She asked me if I would like the article. I said, "Yes, very much." A couple of days later I received the article in the mail, but I could not read it—it was in German. I asked a friend's German-born wife to translate it for me. In essence it just repeated what was stated in the national news regarding the kidnapping.

After the dust of the kidnapping seemed to settle and the fleeting fifteen minutes of fame generated from the Oprah Winfrey Show waned, I had every hope of relegating the kidnapping to the backburner of my life. I was sadly mistaken. I soon discovered that the twisted, distorted tentacles of that heinous crime began to permeate my mind and stir childhood horrors that should have been left sealed deep within my psyche.

Pamela Crabtree

PART II

Pamela Crabtree

Chapter Four
LITTLE ELLIE

I felt his finger go under my panties, and before I could squirm away he had violated me. He did not just penetrate me once, he did it several times, each thrust going further and further up me until my innocence was broken. I begged him to let me down, saying that I did not want to play the game anymore. As he gently put me down, he slowly slid his finger out of my pants and asked me to go for a walk with him in the woods. I was frightened, ashamed, and just wanted to go home and deal with my shame, the enormous shame that only a child of nine would feel.

As I sat on my front porch that bright summer afternoon, I waited, just knowing that that man would come and tell my parents what I had done. He would blame me, and then I would get yelled at and spanked. I was oblivious to the fact that the crime that had been committed was against me.

I knew that what we did was not right, but surely a grown-up could not do anything wrong. Grown-ups were kind and trustful, like my aunts, uncles, neighbors, and even the milkman I saw almost daily throughout my young life in the 1950s.

I frantically peddled my red tricycle down the elm tree-lined sidewalk, barely beating the horse-drawn milk truck before it came to its customary stop at my neighbor's house. The driver was a kind old man wearing a white uniform with hair that matched his uniform. Dropping the reins, he jumped down from the truck, knowing his horse would not gallop away, and awarded me the prize for winning the race. The prize was a chip off the crystal-clear block of ice from the back of his milk truck. To this day, I have never tasted ice so delicious.

My love for animals and my sensitivity for living things were sparked early on and was first noticed with my love for the milkman's horse. Whenever I could, I would take the horse some sugar or carrots. I'd stand on my tiptoes and try to look into his big brown eyes, which were partially covered by blinders. I enjoyed caressing his soft, velvety nose and petting his hairy face that was as long as a child's week.

"How are you today?
Are you enjoying the carrots and sugar?"
I quizzed him as though I expected a reply. He always looked sullen and seemed to have a hint of a tear in his eye. I was sure that my attention would cheer him up, but all he ever did was shake his head up and down and whinny at me.

Back then I was a naive, short, skinny blonde with blue eyes and a cute round face. I was the third of four children, having an older brother and sister—Ken and Julie—and a younger brother, Paul. Ken was three years older than I was, and we shared the only blondeness in the family. We also shared what seemed to be an innate ability, even at a young age, to exude a politeness framed with a charm that not many young people possessed in the 1950s. Ken was a cute little boy, and he and Paul grew to be nice-looking men.

As I look back, Ken and I sure as hell enjoyed a good time. Many times we would be the center of attention at weddings and other parties while dancing the jitterbug together to Glenn Miller's recording of "In the Mood." People would form circles around us and cheer us on. Ken would toss me around like a rag doll. We were pretty agile back then.

Julie, six years my senior, was a dark-haired beauty. There was nothing cute about her, she was pretty. Her personality and temperament, however, mirrored a finely bred cat, in that her aloofness and seriousness masked a massive amount of insecurity and inferiority. Paul, though six years younger than me, seemed to favor the personalities that Ken and I possessed—an outgoing personality surrounded by an aura of charm, but, like our older sister, was haunted with some insecurities. There was no doubt that I absolutely adored my brothers and worshipped my older sister. Until my death, I shall always love my siblings unconditionally.

Though I was in the middle of my sibs, I never felt preoccupied with that position. In spite of being somewhat invisible, I felt contented, carefree, and happy in my early childhood. I was given a free rein at coming and going even at the ripe old age of nine. Boundaries were as unknown in my home as a hug and a kiss. I regularly roamed my neighborhood and its surrounding areas and used my mental map to guide me past the manicured lawns in the affluent Morehouse area. I'd often end my trek by going into the local Catholic Church and offering up a penny so I could light a vigil candle. I knew if I did not pay, my prayer would go unanswered. When I had extra money I'd drop a nickel in the poor box at the rear of the church. Sometimes I'd tried to peak in the coin slit to see how much money was offered to the poor. It never looked like very much. I supposed that the old men and women were saving their money to light a vigil candle so their prayers would be answered.

I was sensitive, empathetic, and loyal. I was athletic, tomboyish, and proud that I could run faster than any kid on my block. I preferred to play with my Roy Rogers gun and holster than the apron-clad sissy doll I received one birthday. However, it amused me when I would press her belly and she would whine, "mama." I liked the dolls that would wet even less—they made such a mess. I also had more fun playing first base on the local park's softball team than playing with Barbie and Ken.

The Gift of Hurt

That I hated to wear dresses would be an understatement. The starchy frilly lace scratched me to no end, especially at the neck and arms. At Christmas and on my birthdays, Aunt Joanne and Uncle Robert always bought me frilly dresses and girl stuff. They were determined to make a little lady out of me. I preferred slacks and jeans, but Mom forced me to wear the girly stuff on special occasions, such as holidays and weddings. Most of the time the frilly, starchy garments met an early demise as they yellowed and wilted in my closet.

I discovered early on that the perceived safety of the 1950s allowed me the freedom to come and go and ride my bike to my favorite place—the local park. I especially loved the park in the spring and summer, when its wintry brown panorama blossomed into numerous shades of green. I found the park to be a pleasant respite from a chaotic home life. However, my haven of peace was violated that summer when I rode by myself to a pond, located in the middle of the park. That violation came in the form of a man who wanted to know if I would like to play a game.

Of course I wanted to play a game, what nine-year-old would not want to play a game? I immediately noticed that the man had an uncanny resemblance to Del Moore, the man who portrayed Betty White's husband on one of my favorite TV shows, *Life with Elizabeth*. I saw him as handsome, fun, and Elizabeth loved him, so this guy must be okay.

In the course of our conversation, I must have mentioned the resemblance because he said he was indeed Betty White's TV husband and was visiting his family in our area. I believed him. I had an immense amount of unconditional trust back then.

The game began when he led me to the end of the wooden dock on the small pond that was home to sunfish, bullheads, and crawfish. He picked me up and pretended to throw me in the pond. He put me down, and we both laughed. I was wearing a T-shirt and shorts. Having gained my trust, he picked me up again, only this time he placed his large hands on my crotch and around my chest and pretended to throw me in the pond again. He did that a few times, and then I felt his finger go under my panties. To this day I remember thinking it must have been a mistake. This time he did not put me down. He nonchalantly continued the game, and then I felt his finger penetrate my vagina.

With each additional thrust he entered me further until I was so frightened I told him I did not want to play anymore. When he finally put me down, he said, "Let's take a walk in woods."

"No, I have to go home."

Thank God I had the presence of mind to tell him no. In spite of what that pedophile did to me, I respectfully said goodbye, ran to my bike, hopped on it, and sped off. The truth was that I did not have to go home. No one was keeping track of my whereabouts.

When I reached the safe haven of my front porch, I waited for my father to angrily summon me. I waited like a death row prisoner for her executioner—praying that the time would never come and yet knowing my doom was near. With slapping, punching, spanking, and humiliation being the regular punishments in our house, I had prepared myself for the confrontation. I deserved it; I had done something dirty. I sat on the porch, waiting, holding my knees like some children would hold their teddy bears, but the inevitable never happened, and I filed that event away in the back of my mind.

As a survival tactic, I learned early on not to make any mistakes or to rock the boat. As I grew, I hungered for attention from Mom and Dad, and I wanted to be a source of pride for them by being a good girl. Unfortunately, my parents were not the kind of people who would sit down and get your side of the story before they doled out punishments. In our house you were guilty until proven innocent, and usually by the time you were found innocent you had already been hit or humiliated.

I longed to be cared for—nurtured if you will—and when I hear the modern term quality time used to describe child-parent relationships, I think of the unusual quality time I shared with my mom when I was a child. It was usually after she and Dad had argued. Instead of sleeping with him, she'd come in my room and sleep in my bed. We'd talk, and then she would scratch my back or my feet. Believe it or not, those were nice times. As a plus, with Mom lying next to me, that meant she would not be picking at Dad, and Dad would not be yelling back.

Another mind-boggling concern was the threat of being humiliated. I pretty much could take any beating or humiliation in our home, when it was just between the disciplining parent and me. However, it nearly destroyed me emotionally when they tried to exorcise their own insecurities and demons by degrading me in public.

One time when I was around twelve-years-old our family rented a cottage, with my dad's sister, Millie, her husband, Ron, and their sons, Billy and Tommy. One morning Tommy and I took my dad's sixteen-foot wooden boat out for a ride. About half-a-mile from the cottage the thirty-five-horsepower Evinrude motor stalled, and Tommy could not get it started again. Back then you'd rap a cord around the top of the motor and yank it with all your might and hope that the motor would start.

Tommy quickly tired from pulling and yanking, and when I tried pulling, my arms gave out after only a few tries. Tommy pulled the propeller shaft up to look at it, and while he was bending over trying to spot the problem his dark-rimmed glasses slipped off his sweaty face, flipped into the water, and quickly sank. Tommy became panic-stricken because he could not see without them. Without thinking he jumped in to try to find them. A minute or so into his futile search he shouted, "Help me find them, will ya?"

"Yeah, sure Tommy."

I jumped into the murky water to join the hunt.

The depth of the water was about ten-feet. While we kept diving down the cold water to feel for his glasses, the boat was drifting away. We had forgotten to throw in the anchor.

While this was happening my uncle was sitting on the porch of the cottage looking through binoculars at us and believing we were in trouble. In his concern for us he put on his funny-looking World War II army-issued bathing cap and swam out to us.

Meanwhile, Tommy and I kept searching the wet blackness, hoping to find his glasses. With hope fading fast, I came up again for a gulp of air and shouted, "Son-of-a-bitch, the boat's gone!"

I paddled around and spotted it. I quickly swam to catch up with it. I struggled up its beveled side, gashing my arm when I fell into the boat and landed on the gas tank. I managed to heave the heavy anchor into the lake and dove back in to help Tommy.

My uncle finally reached us.

"Are you kids OK?"

"Yes, Uncle Ron, Tommy lost his glasses."

"And the motor won't turn over, Dad."

We filled him in on the problem, and he said there was no way in hell we were going to find Tommy's glasses. After my uncle fiddled with the inside of the motor, it started. I guess the problem was with the spark plug or fuel line. We began our drive back to the cottage.

As we got closer to land, I saw my dad waiting there. "Oh, shit, I'm gonna get it now." I know how a trapped animal must feel, because I had nowhere to run. Dad met us on the dock and started to scream at me for goofing around. I tried to explain what had happened, but he was pissed. I do not recall if my uncle tried to reason with him, but I was punished and humiliated and that was that. Tommy never received any type of punishment or reprimand.

The only thing my parents ever accomplished by their humiliation tactics was to instill an immense anger and a lack of self-confidence in me. Paradoxically, it also caused me to have an abnormal attachment to them.

Back then Mom and Dad did not realize it, but they used psychology to punish us. Mom would say, "You kids just wait until your father gets home, you're gonna get it."

And boy did we. Dad was a great one to make us stand in front of him as he took off his belt loop by loop before striking us with it. The suffering of the pending spanking by Dad was sometimes unbearable and sometimes worse than the spanking. I was very much afraid of my father. I always felt that he hit me until he felt better. I would have done anything, anything to avoid his wrath. Sadly, I got to the point where I did do something to avoid his wrath—I began to keep everything inside of me. I never confided my failings or foibles to anyone. If I made a mistake, I'd do anything to cover it up.

Mom, more than Dad, was a screamer, although one time she became very angry with Ken and threw, like a Frisbee, the lid off a newly opened can of vegetables, cutting him just above his eye. In years to come, Mom would verbally admonish her actions to me realizing what could have happened. Ken always excused my parents' actions by saying that he was a bad boy and deserved to be hit. Out of the four of us, it is true that he challenged them much more than the three of us combined. The rest of us were more intimidated by Mom and Dad than Ken was.

One time when he was about sixteen he had an argument with them and ran away from home. No one knew where he had gone until the Florida police called and told my parents that their son and his buddy were being held in an upper Florida jail. The police asked them to wire money so he could take a bus home. Mom sent the money not only for Ken but also for his friend. The other boy's mother refused to send her son any money. During his disappearance I missed Ken very much, and I was terribly worried about him. To this day he'll mention every so often that he remembers I was the only one who seemed to care that he had run away from home. He seems to appreciate the fact that I love him.

Unlike Ken, I always tried to be a source of joy in my parents' not-so-good life. I tried the Eddie Haskell approach with outsiders and was always polite and respectful. Adults ate up that. In school I was well liked, though my grades were far below my abilities. Actually, I thought I did not have the smarts to do well, so I never pushed myself. My parents' only concern regarding school was whether I would pass to the next grade and graduate from high school. Their goals for me were simple and easy to meet: graduate from high school, work at an office job outside of the home until I got married, and then, and only then, have children. Perhaps I interpreted that as thinking I did not have the intelligence to make it in college or the real world.

It puzzles me now when I think back to my elementary and high school years and how I found attending school difficult mainly because it forced me to be away from my mother. I did, however, find some comfort in the security and consistency of grade school—not so much in high school. Interestingly, when we had air raid drills in grade school to prepare us for the dropping of the atomic bomb, it made me feel valued—if I was in school when we were bombed, my teacher felt I was important enough to be saved.

In essence I desperately needed structure, affection, consistency, unconditional love, and peace. I found some of that in school, at my friends' houses, and in the arms of sexual abusers and lovers. My lack of confidence and the hunger for affection and acceptance was to be the precursor to an adolescence filled with sexual promiscuity.

Because I was not monitored and no one really cared what I did, there was no one to stop me from my sexual adventures in alleys and garages with young men from the neighborhood. It was not until years later with the help of two psychotherapists that I realized because of the age difference between the young men who experimented with me that I was really sexually abused. To this day I will always despise those young men.

When I was grown, I read that one of them had died of natural causes. I felt no sadness. Only relief that this person who used me and knew my secret was dead. It's not a nice thought to admit, but that's the way I felt. One other boy who was closer to my age accosted me while I was cleaning up our garage for Dad and tried to force me to have oral sex with him. He came into the garage and casually said, "Hey Ellie, put my dick in your mouth."

"You're sick, Mike, I can't do that."

He pushed me against the wall and started forcing me down, but I pulled away and ran into my house. I never told a soul. A couple of years later a local girl around age thirteen was found murdered in my neighborhood. The murder is still unsolved. I recently found out that the girl died from strangulation when she was forced to have oral sex with the murderer. I often wondered about Mike and what might have happened if I had not gotten away from him. Mike and the murdered girl were acquaintances.

After considerable pondering, I can finally pinpoint when my anger pool began to fill: when I was an innocent seven-year-old and was forced to say goodbye to my dead grandfather. That event turned out to be the start to a protective splitting of my personality. My personality split was not the same as a person with multiple personalities or a schizophrenic; nevertheless, it has caused me considerable difficulties. For instance, I lacked the self-confidence and trust that people could accept me as I was. I always played roles or put on facades. I would be the clean-cut polite girl at school, who frequently would receive an "O" for outstanding citizenship on my grade card and then put on my fun face with my girlfriends when we went out in the evenings and weekends.

I would try to be the goody-goody girl when I dated some boys, yet I knew that if the neighborhood guys would call me I would meet them in the alley or wherever they wanted for a sexual encounter. It got to the point where I could not say no to any of them. I became a teenage nympho. I hated myself and I hated them. I hated them touching me, yet at the same time I loved the feeling their touches aroused in me. I never experienced an orgasm with them, but just the idea that someone wanted me felt good because most of the time I went around feeling inconsequential. My quickie liaisons with these young men lasted only until they were satisfied, then I would go my way and they would go theirs.

This promiscuity led to several sexual exploits as I got older. I remember one time I went out with an army private who was stationed at the local military camp. He took me to a drive-in theater and we started making out. He pushed me down on the seat and said that he loved me and then proceeded to make love to me. He asked me to tell him I loved him and of course I did—it seemed to make everything all right. Another encounter I had with a serviceman, from the same camp, was when we swam out to a raft on the local lake and lay there talking. Of course, that was short-lived. He was after only one thing, and he damn near got it. He only got as far as petting because some other swimmers swam out to the raft and interrupted our passionate foray.

One perceptive dirtbag had me pegged from the start. We double-dated with a friend of mine and her boyfriend and ended up at some old run-down farmhouse. He took me into the barn and started making love to me. I told him, "Stop that, I'm not that kind of girl."

I really did not want to be that kind of girl, especially with him. I picked a horrible time to try to brainwash myself into thinking that I could say no to this wannabe man whose only goal at the moment was to get in my pants.

"Bullshit, you know you love it and want it. You're only putting on airs trying to be a virgin, and you're not good at all."

He was right, I was not a good girl, but I'd be damned if I would let him in my pants. I held my own, although I desperately wanted to make love to him.

Although my home life was anything but peaceful, it did not seem to affect my friendships. I had many friends, but my best friend was Kathy. We met when we were about seven-years-old. She was a short brunette and definitely prettier than me. For the next several years we were inseparable. We even went into the bathroom together, and while she did her job I'd sit on the bathtub and jabber and vice versa. She frequently slept over at my house. Sometimes I would stay at her house, although I preferred staying at my house because I did not like being away from my mother. I always had a problem as a child with homesickness.

Kathy was from England, and I was very fond of her parents, Deborah and Rodger. I also looked up to her older sister, June, and her brother, Anthony. June was a neat person because she treated us like we mattered and were important. We were not just little kids who were in the way. I remember one time Kathy and I memorized the words to "April Love" and sang the whole song to June. She made a big fuss over our rendition of the Pat Boone hit. Anthony, was big, good-looking, and a macho guy. He was a varsity football player who made all-city for the local high school. I remember watching in awe as he ate an entire bologna sandwich in two bites.

Sadly, for Kathy's family, June became pregnant out of wedlock when she was sixteen or seventeen. In the late 1950s that was a horrible embarrassment to the family and an immoral act against society.

Although my parents never said anything to me about June's pregnancy, I found out later that my sister did not care for June because she seemed to be wild. I suppose according to standards of the 1950s she might conceivably be labeled as wild, but according to 1990s standards she was way ahead of her time.

She married her child's father, and they had a healthy baby boy. Kathy and I adored him and would often push his stroller up and down the street. Though June later divorced her husband, she remained a good, loving mother to her only child. He grew up to be a fine man.

During the summer Kathy and I would spend considerable time riding our bikes around our surrounding neighborhood. She rode an English racer with the newly invented hand brakes. My bike was an old fashioned Schwinn coasting bike with the pedal brakes, but it was still a fine blue bike. One of the special places we visited often was Calverton Cemetery. We would walk among the graves and place flowers on some of them. We also made it a point to place flowers on the grave of a twenty-plus-year-old World War II casualty. We spent a lot of time praying by the graves of young people. After our homage to the dead we would sit under a maple tree in the cemetery and eat our lunch of bologna sandwiches, potato chips, and small bottles of Pepsi.

Sometimes we would ride our bikes to the park and race down the death-defying, pot-holed hill located on the golf course. "Come on, Kath, you chicken, watch out for that hole," I'd shout to her. "Meet you at the creek." When I got there, I'd wade into the shallow, muddy creek and try to retrieve some of the golfballs the golfers had lost. Then I'd sell them to the pro shop.

Kathy and I shared not only innocence but also happiness in our youthful friendship that could be witnessed by our laughing camaraderie while we rode our bikes. Along the way we would frequently stop at a weeping willow tree close to the park's entrance. That tree must have been 300 feet high, or so it seemed to us. In reality, the willow tree was maybe thirty feet tall. When we ventured through its green thicket, we entered a magical kingdom that looked like a gigantic room—at least it looked that way to Kathy and me. It was really a clearing around the trunk of the willow tree. We would hide inside and pretend we were all grown up and this was our house.

And a grand house it was until that awful, blue-skied summer day when we entered our magical kingdom and saw an intruder—a man. I did not remember then and I do not remember now what he looked like or what he was wearing. The only thing I remember is that he exposed his penis to us and stood there fondling it. We ran, terrified. The magical kingdom we so enjoyed became a house of filth that we never visited again. To this day Kathy remembers our weeping willow playhouse, but not the exposure incident.

When I was growing up in the mid-1950s television was a new medium. Even though we had a TV set in our front room, it was rarely on. I remember my mother ironing and listening to *Stella Dallas* and *Young Doctor Malone* on the radio. I even have slight recollections of listening to scary stories on the radio like *The Shadow*.

Slowly, I turned away from radio and gravitated toward television. During those early years I looked forward to watching *My Friend Irma* and listening to the squeaky, almost irritating voice of the star of the show, Marie Wilson. Each weekday I would sit on the end of my chair and holler to Mom, "Is it five yet?"

I anticipated the words, "Do you know what time it is? It's Howdy Doody time!"

Buffalo Bob Smith was the first person I ever put up on a pedestal. I laughed at Clarabelle the Clown and thought that Mr. Bluster was a mean man. *The Mickey Mouse Club* was also on each day, and I imagined that I was one of the Mouseketeers. I fell in love with Spin and Marty, the young dude ranch heroes.

I looked forward to the first-run slapstick antics of Lucille Ball on *I Love Lucy*. Late at night—and it did not matter if it was a school night—before signoff and test patterns I would watch roller derby and the late night shows starring Morey Amsterdam and the videos of Les Paul and Mary Ford.

As I began my second decade of life, Kathy and I would go to a rat-trapped movie theater. It was down a block from my parents' service station. The station was called John's Sohio. Back then when you bought your gas for twenty-nine cents a gallon, the attendant would check your car's water, oil, and tire pressure and clean the windshield. It was much more of a customer-oriented business, and you were on a first-name basis with them. One time a customer came in the station and complained while Dad was cleaning off his windshield that he hated, "These Goddamn bugs that dirty up my windshield."

"Be glad that cows don't fly," Dad said.

I still laugh at that one.

The neighborhood rat-trapped theater showed third-, fourth-, and maybe fifth-run movies. But hell, back then we did not care what was first run. Our mothers would give us twenty-five cents each, and that would get us in, buy one bag of salty popcorn, and one cup of Coke or Orange Crush. We usually went to the theater on Sunday afternoons. We always sat in the front row and watched movies starring Dean Martin and Jerry Lewis or Abbot and Costello. I anticipated the Francis the Talking Mule series with Donald O'Connor. But I especially loved movies starring Roy Rogers or the Bowery Boys. Kathy and I were anxious for the previews of coming attractions and the cartoons that followed them. To this day, I miss that old tradition. You never see the cartoons of Popeye or Casper the Friendly Ghost on movie screens now.

The rat-trapped theater was filthy and filled with many misfits and perverts. The owner and manager was a nasty old man who had no patience for children. If we were making too much noise, he would stop the movie, turn the lights on and yell, "Be quiet or I won't run the movie."

Too bad he never monitored the safety of his patrons. I remember going into the theater's dirty, mauve-colored bathroom, and while I was in the stall doing my business I looked up and there was a woman staring down at me. It scared the hell out of me. I quickly pulled up my panties and slacks, but before running out of the bathroom, she grabbed me and roughed me up. I never told anyone.

Not having learned my lesson, I ventured into the still filthy bathroom months later. This time while doing my business, I saw a man trying to look under the stall. I screamed, "What are you doing?"

I jumped up, zipped up my slacks, but before I could leave he pushed me up against the wall and started to fondle me. I was able to break his hold and duck under his arm. I ran back to my seat and once again never told anyone. I still wonder if he was ever reported or caught by someone who had more guts than me.

When there was a first-run movie we wanted to see, Kathy and I would go downtown and pay the high prices of $1 and sometimes $1.25 the better theaters demanded, but we were able to sit in the comfort and cleanliness of those theaters. They showed movies like *Around the World in 80 Days* or *The Vikings*. We would take the bus downtown, see the movie, have a lunch of macaroni and cheese and coleslaw at a local department store, and then catch the community bus home.

Chapter Five
A VISIT WITH THE DEAD

Preceding the victimization I was subjected to in the mid-1950s, the beginning of the end of my carefree days began when I was about seven-years-old. It was triggered by my grandfather's fatal heart attack in 1953. That night, my father phoned my older sister, who was baby-sitting us and said, "I'm going to pick you kids up - you need to say goodbye to grandpa."

Julie was aware of the severity of the situation and made Ken and me kneel down and pray for our grandfather. I remember obeying her but feeling really dumb. I looked at Ken out of the corner of my eye and returned the smirk he was giving me.

When we reached my grandparents' house, which was always a source of enjoyment for me, I saw my mother crying. I was escorted to the back bedroom, where they had placed grandfather after he collapsed. I was told to go in and say goodbye. I stood outside the bedroom and saw that the blinds had been closed; the room was dimly lit. I took a step forward to enter the room and then hesitated. I did not want to go in; I wanted to go home. All of a sudden, there was a hand clasped around my wrist, tugging me toward my grandfather's dead body. When I saw my grandfather's white stocking feet at the headboard, I broke the sweaty hold and ran into the bathroom, locked the door, and huddled in the corner next to the bathtub.

I cried and stayed in that corner for what seemed liked hours. After composing myself, I cautiously unlocked the door and peeked out the corner to see if anyone waited outside for me. No one was there. I made my getaway to the living room, where I commandeered the footstool and quietly sat. I did not want to be conspicuous and at that moment would not have yelled if I had been stuck with a pin.

The house was abuzz with strangers.

"What's that coming at me? That funny bed on rollers and that strange guy pulling it." They said it is my grandpa, and they covered him with a blanket, just like in the movies. I covered my face with an edition of *Look Magazine* as his body passed in front of me.

The days following my grandfather's death were emblazoned in my memory because I spent a significant amount of time at the mortuary, staring at his corpse. He was buried in his dark, wide-lapel, double-breasted suit. His shiny black hair was combed straight back, and he clenched a rosary in his hands. He was fifty-eight-years old.

During the couple of days' visitation, we would leave the mortuary for an hour or so and eat dinner out. Ordinarily, we never dined out as a family. Although I was very sad, I remember how nice it was to be with my family. I even enjoyed spending time with them at the mortuary. They were forced into giving me considerable attention during that time because things can get very monotonous and boring during death vigils.

The day of the funeral, I looked out the sunroom window and saw a black limousine pull up in front of our house. I ran to Ken and shouted, "I get the jumpseat, you can sit next to Dad."

It was really neat in the limo, but I could have done without the lengthy High Mass, which was held in my grandpa's parish church. The pungent odor of incense nauseated me then, and as an adult I still find it offensive.

It was a horribly sad time for my mother. I found out as I grew older that she was particularly fond of her father. She cried a lot after my grandfather died, especially when Eddie Fisher sang "Oh Mein Papa." I was very devoted to my mother and loved her very much. I would not be able to comprehend the pain she experienced until some fifteen-years later.

Chapter Six
A GOOD FRIEND

When my grandfather died, I was only in the first grade, and had not met my dear friend Kathy yet. When we were introduced, we did not even go to the same school. Her parents sent her to a Catholic parochial school. I attended public school.

I thought Kathy was above average intellectually. As for me, I was never an A student, not even a B student. I guess if you averaged my grades in elementary and high school I would have been a very low C student, and lucky to have that C.

As I matured, it became increasingly difficult to follow in my older sister's footsteps because she grew to be so pretty with her petite stature and long brunette hair. I was always relieved when I was not assigned the same teachers Julie had had. Compared to me she was a good student.

One situation that pretty much cinched in my childhood psyche that I was stupid was when I was attending a Girl Scout meeting at the Lutheran Church located across the street from my elementary school. I must have been in fourth or fifth grade, and I overheard one of the leaders refer to me as "backward." That horrible word meant "stupid" to me. I even entertained the thought that I was retarded. I think it did irreparable damage to my self-esteem. It took over forty years and a lot of positive reinforcement before I began to believe that I was intelligent. It is interesting that Kathy never thought of herself as a very good student either. I guess we were a good match because we both lacked self-confidence. Perhaps it was that lack of confidence that allowed us to understand one another and try to take life with a grain of salt and a sense of humor.

As the years went by, Kathy and I became even closer. We could talk about anything and everything. When the toils of school were over, we were together playing jacks or, in the winter, sledding down hills. At the end of the day, we would walk each other to a midpoint between our houses where there was a crack in the sidewalk. Just before we parted we would shake off all the cooties we had accumulated during the day, leave them in the crack in the sidewalk, and retreat to our homes free from any cootie contamination.

When we were finishing up sixth grade, Kathy told me that she and most of her family, meaning her mom, dad, and brother, were moving back to England. June remained in the states with her new husband and their son. Kathy and I were very sad but agreed to write. Damn, we were resilient back then.

Happily, about a year later, I received a letter from her saying that they would be returning to the States and would live on the north side of town with

June and her family. A few weeks later, I received a telephone call from her saying she was back in town. We reunited and picked up right where we left off. The separation had done little to daunt our friendship.

When my mother did not drive me to spend the weekend at Kathy's house or pick Kathy up to spend the weekend with me we would take the bus to each other's house. Her parents and sister did not drive, and rarely would her brother-in-law drive her to my house.

We had a great year attending her volleyball games or my majorette parades. As an adult, she told me how much she enjoyed tagging along with mom and me to the parades around the Midwest area. I was a majorette in a new and upcoming baton twirling corps. My brother Paul was flag bearer. It was a neat time in my life. I loved the short, black uniform with a golden crest embroidered on the chest. I enjoyed listening to the clicking of the toe and heel plates on the bottom of my hightop white boots. I basked in the attention that we got when we marched in local and regional parades.

Being a majorette took a lot of work because we practiced Tuesdays and Thursdays from 6 to 8 p.m. all year long. In the summer we had what was called summer camp. During summer camp we would practice daily from 8 a.m. to 5 p.m. for two consecutive weeks. When I was about fifteen, I resigned from the Corps because I thought I was too old to continue as a majorette. I was finishing up my freshman year in high school. I remember that I wanted to become a majorette in high school, but when I signed up I was told that every majorette had to be able to play an instrument. I was not qualified.

The spring before I started high school, it happened again. Kathy told me she and her parents were moving back to England at the end of her eighth-grade year. We were sad but agreed to stay in touch. She left when we were both about fourteen-years-old. We kept in touch, though as time went on our correspondence became less frequent. It came to pass that Kathy's brother, Anthony, took a position as a police officer in Vancouver, British Columbia. He asked Kathy if she wanted to move with him. She did. While Kathy experienced the life of an avant-garde young student, first in England and then in Vancouver, I was coping with high school life in the States.

For the most part, high school was uneventful, until one day when I arrived at school and heard the buzz.

"Did you hear Brenda killed herself?"
"What!"
"Yeah, she took an overdose because her boyfriend ditched her."

Brenda was cute and petite with short blonde hair. I attended grade school with her, and although we had grown apart in high school we remained friends. Sad, very sad.

Another tragedy in my young life was when another friend who was sensitive, kind and aspired to become a priest, went into his bedroom closet, put the barrel of a shotgun in his mouth, and pulled the trigger. I never found out why he did it. My little brother, Paul, called him the "magic man" because he always had time to stop and show Paul slight-of-hand magic tricks. A tragic ending for a sensitive, troubled, seventeen-year-old boy.

After adjusting to life without Kathy, I ran around with my other, less close friends. One time I skipped school with one of them. But I was so paranoid and frightened during my day of hiding and smoking the Lucky Strike cigarettes I stole from my dad that I never skipped school again. Actually, I did not have to skip school because I pretty much could stay home whenever I wanted.

My parents never paid too much attention to my school years. As long as I passed to the next grade and the school principal or teachers never called them they were satisfied. One time, in grade school, I asked Mom and Dad to attend a concert our choir was going to give around Christmas. I proudly announced, "I get to sing solo, and I'd really like you guys to come and see me."

Mom, my grandmother, and Julie attended. Other than that concert, the only time my parents entered my school was to see me graduate or when they voted.

My parents sent extremely mixed messages to me. For instance, they bought a 1956 bright red Ford Crown Victoria for me when I was a sophomore in high school. I was ecstatic. Yet, when I needed them emotionally—like when my friends committed suicide—I received no understanding and was expected to tough it out. It was like, oh well, let that be a lesson to you.

Another confusing (albeit profitable) situation for me was when I would pick up a few of my friends to go out for the evening and stop at my dad's service station to get $2 worth of gas (all the girls pitched in fifty cents). Dad would come out and kid around with all of us and then fill the tank up and not charge me. It goes without saying that at that particular moment I was proud of my dad and appreciated it mainly because it showed a different, kinder side of him. It was a charming, softer side he did not show very often in private, but would often show around outsiders.

My parents believed that children were to be seen and not heard. We were to be polite and respectful to our elders, and our feelings were never, ever considered. We were never to question adult authority figures. Adults knew best.

After I graduated from high school, I moved with my parents to a new home in a local suburb. I was thrilled with the new house. What was really neat is that the new house had a shower. The old house only had a bathtub.

That summer in 1964 I secured my first job as a secretary in the pharmacy at a local hospital. I hated it almost immediately when I found out that I had to work holidays. I also discovered that it became increasingly difficult being away from my mother. I suppose what I was suffering from would be something like separation anxiety. More than likely it had been triggered by the move to a new house and leaving the familiar high school environment.

To aggravate an already unhappy situation, I had to battle the constant sexual advances and innuendoes by a middle-aged pharmacist named Mr. Riley. I was being sexually harassed before it became known as such. He insisted that I fill prescriptions and floor supplies—which consisted of replenishing many medications for the nurses stations throughout the hospital. I remember how accessible Seconal, Nembutal, Demerol, and other addictive medications and barbiturates were for me. I knew right where the key to the cabinet was, and I would access it frequently while filling prescriptions. But I was never even tempted.

Meanwhile, Mr. Riley continued his crusade of harassment against me by making lewd suggestions and talking vulgarly. The last straw was when he unzipped the back of my uniform. I went to the department supervisor, Sister Mary Alan. She was a brilliant woman, but when I told her what Mr. Riley was doing to me, she offered no consolation or assistance. She left me with the impression that pharmacists were harder to come by than secretaries, so I should grin and bear it.

I began to miss work and ultimately resigned my position from the hospital. After that, I worked at a local department store as a cashier. That was not a good experience either. I found myself being dominated and allowing men to intimidate me there, too. Back then, men were the bosses, plain and simple, and it certainly did not help to be raised in an atmosphere that cultivated the belief that men were the superior gender.

A few months into my tenure at the department store I was offered a position as a cashier at a drugstore. The owner said that he would pay me five cents more than minimum wage to start, and I accepted the position. I was making $1.30 an hour, and it was great! I really enjoyed my job. I liked the people I worked with and the interaction with most of the customers. Granted, it was not big money, but then I was a woman.

Chapter Seven
THE FALL BEGINS

A few months before we moved to the new house, I met a young man by the name of Matt. He was eighteen, portly, blond with green eyes and a smile that drove me wild. It was the most contagious smile I have ever seen. He worked for a department store in their package pickup and made a whopping $1.65 an hour. We met at a fishing pond in a local park, the same pond where I was sexually abused as a nine-year-old. This time, however, I was seventeen and no one was going to abuse me again.

"My God, no! Please God, say it's not true."

"Tell me that it was not President Kennedy that was shot. Maybe it was Connors or Johnson, but not President Kennedy. What will happen to Jackie and John and Caroline?"

" Please, God, tell me he'll be all right."

I soon heard that President Kennedy was not all right. I tried as hard as I could to cope with the grief, but at times it was overwhelming. All I did was sit in front of the TV and grieve with Jackie in Texas and all the way to Arlington National Cemetery—where our beloved president was buried.

Two weeks passed, and I was still reeling from the assassination. To try and forget, if only for a little while, I went to the park to watch the ice skaters negotiate their rhythmic moves on the frozen pond. There was a huge bonfire with benches and logs around it. Up on the snow-covered hill vendors sold hot chocolate and coffee. The setting was very nice, like something out of Currier and Ives.

Initially I had been attracted to a close friend of Matt's by the name of Adam. It proved to be a superficial affection, and one that was not returned. I was impressed because Adam was a student at the local university. He also worked for McDonald's, the hamburger place. What was really neat was whenever I went into McDonald's, when he worked, he always shoved an extra order of fries or hamburger in my bag. Now how could I not have affection for this guy?

Matt, Adam, and a boy called Casey (his real name was Jack) hung around together. Casey was a short, stumpy-looking character who tried to make up for his small size with a big mouth. I believe he was the type of boy you could say had a Napoleon complex. He was a typical Fonzie type (although Fonzie had a personality). He took great pride in stealing condoms from the drugstore where he worked and handing them out to his buddies.

Then there was Matt. He seemed nice, too nice to hang around Casey and some of the other guys. When we met at a bonfire, he asked me a bunch of questions about myself, "How old are you?"

"Seventeen."

"Where do you go to school?"

"Washington High."

I asked him questions too.

"How old are you."

"Eighteen."

"What high school did you go to?"

"I graduated from Concorse."

When he told me that he wanted to show me a picture of his best girl, I thought, *What a dork to show me a picture of another girl.* The picture turned out to be his mother. I have to admit I thought it was kind of hokey, but it proved to be an excellent icebreaker.

When I told him I would be eighteen in a couple of months, he offered to show me the town (meaning the bars). I said okay. However, when my birthday came around, I went out with a bunch of girls rather than Matt. Nevertheless, he still pursued me.

We started dating regularly after my eighteenth birthday. He was very affectionate and usually a gentleman, although there were times when he did get fresh. I tried to hold off as long as possible before giving in to him. There was no doubt that I wanted to make love to him, but I was scared to death I would get pregnant. So we usually petted, though one time he did get me into the back seat of his 1958 Chevrolet Biscayne. I recall it like it was yesterday. When the evening started we bought a Chef Boyardee pizza—you know the kind that comes with all the ingredients in a box. You have to mix the pizza dough and let it rise and then form it into a circle and top it with pizza sauce, cheese, and so on.

We fixed the pizza at my house and then went out for a ride in his Chevy. He and his buddies all drove 1958 Chevys. He drove to the closest park and stopped by a secluded area around the tennis courts. After kissing and petting, we maneuvered ourselves into the backseat. The windows became fogged up, and as we were in the throes of passion there was a knock on the window. I panicked, and my first thought was that it was my dad. Matt exclaimed, "Jesus Christ!" It turned out to be a couple of police officers.

"Get out of the car"

"What are you doing here?"

"We were making out," snapped Matt.

"Any drinking going on?"

"No," was our simultaneous answer.

One of the cops spotted the bag the pizza came in.

"What's this?"

"The bag from pizza"

"Oh, pizza comes in a bag like this?"

We started to explain that it was a Chef Boyardee pizza. The cop interrupted and started asking us more questions.

"How old are you?

"Where do you go to school?"

We answered his questions. I was terrified that he would take us to the police station and call my father.

He told us to get out of the park. Matt started the car and drove off, but instead of leaving the park he drove further into the park and stopped at another make-out point and started to kiss me again.

"Forget it," I snapped. "I'm still shook up over the cops; I'm not going to chance it again." Frustrated he drove me home.

I found out later in our relationship that when I would not give in to him he would go to girls/women who would indulge him. When I found out how promiscuous he was, I was really hurt. I guess I believed what was good for the goose was not good for the gander.

Our dating years turned out to be turbulent times. I had to put Matt through the paces before I really believed he loved me. I was emotionally immature and could not handle the love that Matt showed me and expected in return. I was suspicious, jealous, and lacked trust. Nevertheless, he must have seen something in me because he hung around. We agreed that we would not get married until Matt secured a better-paying job. In the spring of 1965 he got a better paying job, and the first thing he did was purchase an engagement ring and wedding band for me.

I was delighted, as were my parents. However, Matt's parents were less than pleased. Paramount in their minds was the fact that I was Catholic and Polish, a religion and nationality they found hard to accept. To complicate matters further, not only were my future in-laws Mason and Eastern Star members but Matt had just been promoted to master counselor of the DeMolays, the small-time version of the Masons. That office was the equivalent of being president of an organization or club. When the bigwigs at Matt's dad's Masonic Temple got wind that Matt was dating a Catholic girl they called a special meeting, summoned Matt's father, and insisted that he do something to break us up. Matt and his father talked; however, Matt made it known to everyone that as soon as we could we were going to be married. His father respected his decision and lived with the flack. The whole deal put Matt's parents in a terribly embarrassing position. That was not our intention. We were just two young people deeply in love wanting to start a new life together.

Matt's mother took everything very badly and pressured Matt incessantly about breaking up with me. All her nagging accomplished was to push him closer to me. He ended up resigning his chair as master counselor. It was an ugly ending.

I was well aware that mixed marriages in the Catholic Church were not tolerated or allowed, and I told Matt from the beginning that I had no intention of going against the practices of the church. I asked him to attend mass with me one Sunday. He did and did not much care for it.

"Would you talk with a favorite priest of mine, Matt?"

"Yes."

Father Pitts was very patient and kind and explained some of the beliefs of the Catholic faith to Matt.

On the one side, I began a full-court press to try and convert Matt to Catholicism. On the other side, his mother was pressuring him to stay Lutheran. It became a volley between his mother and me with poor Matt in the middle. One day my mother said, "Stop putting Matt in such a difficult position. The more you nag, the more he'll resist."

I followed my mother's advice and quit pressuring him. Meanwhile his mother continued to nag him and in doing so, pushed him over to my side. After attending church with me several more times, he seriously considered converting to the Catholic faith. In order to be accepted into the Church, back then, you had to complete catechism lessons and then be baptized. When his mother found out about the baptism, she called Father Pitts and reamed him out.

"What kind of parents do you think we are?" "We had Matt baptized when he was an infant."

"I'm sure you are good parents. It will be a conditional baptism into the Catholic faith."

Nevertheless, she was livid, and her prejudice against Catholics exacerbated the situation.

In 1965 Matt converted and was baptized conditionally into the Catholic faith. He asked my Uncle Robert to be his godfather. Uncle Robert accepted the honor. Uncle Robert is my godfather as well.

Matt gave me an engagement ring in June 1965. The first thing we did was ask Father Pitts to bless our engagement and wedding rings. He performed the ceremony at the communion rail inside the Church.

We started to plan our wedding and made the subsequent reservations and put a deposit down on the hall. Our marriage would take place in April, 1966 in the local Catholic Church. There would be a breakfast immediately following the Saturday morning wedding ceremony and a reception that evening in the Veterans' Hall.

However, the summer of 1965 proved traumatic for us after Matt received a greeting from Uncle Sam saying that he would be bused to Cleveland to undergo a physical for possible induction into the army. What added insult to injury is that when he graduated from high school in 1963 he signed up for the Navy, but they

Pamela Crabtree

rejected him because he was overweight. He very much wanted to serve his country in the Navy. Several of the men in his family were Navy veterans.

Matt and I were placed in a difficult position because we were in the midst of planning our wedding, and now faced the threat that he may have to serve two years in the army and most likely be sent to Vietnam. We talked the situation over, and Matt decided to enlist in the National Guard. The way the Guard was set up is that you serve six months of active duty and thereafter a weekend a month and two weeks a summer for several years. It was ideal, as he would still be able to serve his country and we could keep our planned wedding date.

When he went to enlist in the Guard, he was told that he would be placed on a waiting list. We were very upset and frustrated because we wanted to do the honorable thing and yet we desperately wanted to get married. The Guard gave him no definitive time frame of when they would call him—it could be in six months or even a year. Being married or a full-time student guaranteed a military deferment back in the early 1960s. Matt had tried the student game, but that turned out to be a horrendously bad choice because he found that he could not work full time in addition to overtime and still carry a full load at the local university. There was absolutely no way he could quit his factory job and give his studies the complete attention they deserved. The only way we could stay together was by getting married.

Then, in midsummer 1965, a declaration by President Johnson stated that men who were married after the end of July or the end August 1965 would not be able to use marriage as a deferment for avoiding the draft. What that Johnson declaration really meant is you better get married before the end of July, because if you did not you were going to be drafted and sent to Vietnam.

In a panic, we contacted Father Pitts and asked him to perform the marriage ceremony immediately. He tried to calm us down, but he knew that we were serious about eloping. He asked us to wait until after Matt's army physical. Before bidding us goodbye he said, "Call me before you go out-of-state to get married."

Many couples were rushing off to get married before the Johnson cut-off date, including some of our friends.

After we calmed down and began to think logically, we reluctantly decided to take our chances and hoped that the National Guard would come through. We did not want to start off our marriage thinking the only reason we married was so Matt could dodge the draft.

The sun was just coming up. Through the redness in the sky it looked as though it was going to be a beautiful day the morning on the day Matt left for his physical. I packed him a bag lunch and drove him down to the government center to wait for the bus that would transport him and thirty or forty other boys to Cleveland.

When he returned that evening he complained, "All it was most of the day was hurry, hurry and then wait, wait, wait."

"We walked around in our jockey shorts with a nametag and a bag holding our valuables around our neck."

Matt and I waited, terrified, for his selective service classification. A few weeks later he received a letter saying that the government had listed him 1-Y because of albumin in his blood. We were relieved, although bittersweetly so. His health concerned me. Nevertheless, we were able to go ahead with the wedding plans.

Each step of planning the wedding went on as scheduled. I would acquiesce to every one of my parents' requests regarding the arrangements. I suppose you could even say it was their wedding because Matt and I were just puppets for everyone. When they said jump, we would jump. I recall that I very much wanted my new sister-in-law, Grace, in the wedding as one of my bridesmaids. My mother overruled my request saying that because Grace was pregnant and would be showing, it would be unseemly to have her in the wedding party. I fought it fiercely but finally relinquished to my mother's demand after she said she would not pay for the wedding if Grace was in it. We were also getting considerable flack from Matt's side of the family.

I believe that if Matt and I had been older, more mature, and self-confident, we would have told everyone in no uncertain terms to go straight to hell and not only would Grace have been in our wedding but there would have been other changes, too. But we both were so young, unsure, and inexperienced that everyone usually got his or her way.

April 1966, was a beautiful day for a wedding—sunny as can be, with the clear blue sky setting off my full-length white wedding gown. Matt was handsome in his formal attire of tails and ascot. It was a dream come true.

I cried uncontrollably when I said my part of the wedding vows. I cried again at our reception when it came time for the unveiling. In an old Polish tradition, the mother of the bride removes the veil of her daughter and replaces it with a funny cap signifying that the mother gives her daughter to her new husband—to begin doing wifely duties for him.

The Sunday following the wedding we left for a two-week honeymoon that started in Washington, D.C., and ended in Ft. Lauderdale, Florida. It was a wonderfully carefree time, just the two of us—no parents, no criticisms, just fun—two twenty-year-olds desperately in love and anticipating our new life together.

When we returned from our honeymoon to what we thought was a beautiful one-bedroom apartment, there was a telegram waiting for Matt that informed him that his factory was on strike. He was to report for strike duty a couple of days later. Luckily, I still had my job as a cashier at the drugstore, and we had few hundred dollars in the bank. After a short duration the strike was settled, and Matt returned to his job as a die setter at the factory.

Lo and behold, four months after our marriage, I found out I was pregnant. We were delighted. Shortly after, I quit my job and, as we had discussed before our marriage, I began my career as a stay-at-home mom.

It was good that I had decided to quit my job before the baby was born because I was so sick I could not work. My obstetrician put me on morning sickness pills and much to my pleasure, the nausea and vomiting went away.

One morning after I drove Matt to work I visited Grace. As we were having coffee at her kitchen table I felt the weirdest sensation of my head being pulled over to the right. I was talking when I felt my lower lip being pulled down also to the right. I tried to act like nothing was happening, but I started to become anxious and told Grace I should get home. By the time I arrived at home my head and my mouth had a more pronounced pull to the right, and my fingers began to tighten up at the joints.

I was horribly frightened. I did not know what was happening. I had to pick Matt up at work at 5 p.m. By that time I was crippled. I could hardly make it to the car; driving was very risky, but I persevered and made it to his office. I lay on the front seat, and when Matt came out he could hardly believe what he saw. He told me later that he thought, "Oh my God, is she going to stay that way the rest of her life?"

He rushed me home and onto the couch and immediately called my obstetrician. I was crippled from head to toe. I could not straighten up at all; my whole body was in a contorted position. Fortunately, I did not experience any pain.

The doctor told Matt to calm down and that he would call back in a few minutes. When the doctor finally called back an hour or so later, he said that he had been reading up on what was happening to me and found out that I was experiencing an allergic reaction to the medication Compazine—my morning sickness pills. He said it would not affect the baby and that I was to drink a lot of liquids so the Compazine would flush out of my system. I, of course, did what the doctor said and about 11 p.m. the crippling affects began to subside. By the middle of the night I was back to normal, and all the affects of the medicine had worn off. I never took the medicine again. Of course, the morning sickness returned, but it only lasted a couple of more weeks and then it was gone.

My son Randy was born on April 30, 1967. It was a very difficult birth, and I was in labor for a long time. I had established a good rapport with my obstetrician and adored him. I had complete faith in him as far as my medical care was concerned. However, as I was to find out later, my mother did not have that same faith, and when I had been in labor for what she viewed as an excessively long time, she called him, yelled at him, and told him he had better do something for me. When I found out what she had done, I was very embarrassed.

"I'm sorry doctor."

"Don't be concerned, she's a mom and was worried about you."

She may have been worried, but she was also drinking and her thinking and acting out were irrational.

After Randy was born, I was placed in a semi-private room and was shocked to see Mom come in. She asked how I was doing and then kissed my dry, chapped lips and left. Her presence and kiss added to my already-present elatedness at being a new mom.

Randy was born, and everyone was proud and relieved. One pressing problem was that Matt and I needed to move into a larger apartment or preferably a house, where Randy would have his own room. For the time being we set his crib up in our bedroom, but that posed several problems. Being a first-time mother, every sound or move the baby made would wake me.

"Matt, don't do that, Randy's right there."

Words Matt heard numerous times. I did not want to make love to Matt with Randy right there next to us. On the upside, I loved having Randy so close because I could watch over him so nothing bad happened to him. It was so cute when I would wake up and roll over to peek at him, only to see those two beautiful blue eyes meeting mine.

We did not have enough money for a down payment on a house, so my in-laws offered to let us move in with them until we could save up the remainder of our down payment. We reluctantly agreed. Before we moved in, the four of us sat down and talked about what each couple would be responsible for each month. It was agreed that because I was at home with Randy and my mother-in-law worked, I would keep the house clean. We would split the cost of the groceries.

My mother always maintained a neutral position regarding my in-laws. I understood her concern regarding the move. She felt that I was starting to bond and get to know them, and thought that the move could jeopardize our relationship. She always liked Matt's parents. She said on more than one occasion, "Be good to your in-laws because they're Matt's parents."

It was only when I told her we were going to move in with them that she voiced to me that she felt it was not a good idea.

I knew the reason she wanted me to be considerate of them. It was because my sister's husband treated mom and dad so badly. They did not deserve the treatment he doled out to them. Mom and Dad respected him, and from what I remember and what I saw, Mom and Dad were very generous to them.

Unfortunately, my mother was right. The six months we lived with my in-laws proved to be a horrible time for me. It was compounded by the fact that my mother-in-law and I were not particularly fond of one another—that was to come later. My mother-in-law adored Randy and Matt. I felt like an outsider. It aggravated the situation when I saw her treat Matt like a little boy. She would drop everything and get him a cup of coffee. It was difficult for me to see her mother him, dote on him, and take his side when we bickered and then be expected to climb into bed and make love to him. It just did not work, and so our love making quickly came to a halt.

In record time we saved enough money for the down payment on a ranch house half-a-mile from my parents' home. Shortly after moving in our new home, Matt suffered an aortic aneurysm. He initially went in the hospital to have his gallbladder removed, but when the surgeon opened him up, he saw an aneurysm. It was a terrifying ordeal. My in-laws were there, as was my younger brother, Paul. We were able to find a few vacant chairs amid the packed surgical waiting room. We waited for the three-hour operation to conclude. It was supposed to be over by noon. Around 3 p.m. as we sat in the almost empty waiting room, Matt's anesthesiologist came out of surgery to inform us about the aneurysm and the seriousness of the situation. He said that the surgeon needed to remove the aneurysm rather than the gallbladder. He went on to describe in detail what an aneurysm was and what was happening to Matt. He finished by saying, "Matt is going to need numerous pints of blood. If anyone in your family could donate-it would help. You can see him when the surgery is over. It would be wise for you to stay here in the hospital."

I stood there, shocked, and he started to walk away. Just as he got to the doorway, I pulled him aside and said, "Are you telling me that my husband may die?"

"If he makes it through the night, more than likely he will live."

I was four months pregnant with our daughter Beth.

The hospital suggested calling a priest. I called the priest at the new parish we had joined when we bought our new home. He coldly said, "The hospital will provide a chaplain to administer extreme unction if he needs it."

You bastard, was my feeling. That rejection was the beginning of the end for my deep belief in priests. I did not call Father Pitts because he was no longer our parish priest. However, he did come up unannounced and unrequested. Father Pitts was a wonderful man and my saving grace. He was the reason I hung on to the Catholic religion.

Thank God, Matt made it through the night. What the doctors ended up doing was replacing part of his aorta with a plastic, Y-shaped valve. Matt was in the intensive care unit for a week. It was a week he still cannot remember, but it is embedded in my mind as clearly as the sexual abuse in the park. After leaving the ICU, Matt remained in the hospital another week or so. It was great to see him regain his strength, although it was a slow process. I remember how excited we would get when they starting taking out the tubes. First the catheter, then the oxygen, then the IVs.

Less than twenty years later, in the mid 1980s, he had to have the plastic valve replaced. This time they put in a graph that was made from a Teflon fabric. It is suppose to hold for twenty-five-years. We'll see.

Before Matt's surgery, I had the opportunity to bask in the pleasure from the wonderful way my mother took to Randy. She was a big help during my recuperation and my early weeks of new motherhood. She even bathed Randy for the first time. I remember, even now, how grateful and amazed I was the day after I came home from the hospital and she came over and fixed a great dinner for Matt and me, all the while taking care of Randy!

I visited my mother a lot during Randy's first months of life. She received such joy from feeding him and playing with him. One poignant moment that I will always remember was the time I put Randy in for a nap on my parents' bed. When he woke up and started to fuss, Mom went in and bounced the bed with her hands and watched as Randy giggled and giggled as he bounced. Mom talked to him, and cooed at him, "You little monkey," she said.

We both laughed, and then she looked up at me. Her smile turned into a frown and she said, "You know Julie would never let me do this to her kids. She would be really mad if I called them monkeys."

Julie was always oversensitive where her husband and children were concerned. I was glad I could give my mother these moments of happiness with Randy.

Dad, on the other hand, was less emotional. When I brought Randy home from the hospital, he stopped in to see the baby for the first time. It was one of the few times he ever visited our apartment. Though I would have liked to see him while I was in the hospital, he never came up to visit me. At that time, mothers were kept in the hospital for five days. The first thing dad said when he looked into the bassinet was, "He's ugly."

"He is not, Dad."

Some daughters might be offended, but I knew my dad, and this was his way of showing he loved the little fellow. Dad indeed loved him. Many mornings, after we moved into our new house, Dad would stop over to see Randy and bring him a chocolate bar. Dad loved all his grandchildren very much, and though it was difficult for him to verbalize it, he showed it by always carrying candy bars in the back pocket of his trousers. All the grandchildren knew right where to go—even little Randy crawled up to his grandpa.

Chapter Eight
MOM, DAD, AND GRANDMA, TOO

As the months progressed, my relationship with my parents began to change for the better. They began to treat me with a new respect and appreciation because I chose to share my life after marriage with them. Mom enjoyed hunting for mushrooms in the country in the fall, and Randy and I would go with her and wait in the car. I did not particularly like mushrooming; I just wanted to be with Mom.

Sundays became a special time for my family, sans my sister and her family. We would all arrive at my parents' home around 1 p.m., grandchildren in tow. Mom would serve us a delicious meal, and then we would just enjoy one another's company. We played softball, swam in Paul's little pool, or took turns on a bike, maneuvering over an obstacle course we had put together. It was great fun and filled with good memories. No fighting or insults, just a family beginning to enjoy and appreciate one another—long overdue.

Sadly, my sister chose not to participate in many of our family doings. Her relationship with my parents was strained at best because my brother-in-law never cared for my parents. His attitude, I believe, influenced my sister's view of our parents. It took me thirty-two-years, but I finally recognized that she had a whole slew of personal demons within her and she must have felt that by ostracizing all of us, she could make those demons go away. I hope she was successful.

As time went on my parents eased up on us and started to respond favorably and with significant relief because they knew that they had raised four fine children. What began to happen now was a mutual exchange of love and respect. They began to treat us as capable and respectable people, as adults, instead of talking down to us.

In spite of their obvious efforts, there seemed to be a certain amount of tension between my older brother, Ken, and my parents because he worked for them at the service station. As hard as they all tried, they could not be completely free from the problems of the business. But an effort was made not to dwell on it too much.

When Mom and Dad bought the service station from my grandmother in the late 1950s it was a thriving business. However, its location soon went down hill, as it became a blighted, high-crime area. In the early 1960s the regular customers began moving out of the neighborhood because it was becoming unsafe. I remember on more than one occasion my father and brothers going to the station in the middle of the night because the police called and said the burglar alarm was going off. Nevertheless, some loyal, die-hard customers patronized the business while my parents continued to try to keep the business solvent.

My mother kept the books, and it seems if she was not paying taxes and Social Security for the company, she was trying to get payment for checks that had bounced. She was an excellent businessperson, more so than my father. I heard her say on more than one occasion that Dad should have kept his factory job. He resigned there to help my grandfather and learn the service station business. Big mistake!

Chapter Nine
THE FALL CONTINUES

My parents were perceived as fun-loving individuals, well liked and respected in the community. Very few people knew of the demons that had plagued them. My father was a handsome man, about five-feet-nine with a medium build. He had a crop of thick black wavy hair. My mother was a pretty woman. She stood about five-feet-four and was somewhat chunky. She had dark brown hair. Though Mom was pretty, her face was scarred because of the horrendous acne she suffered while growing up. She told me that she ate too many sweets and would break out in pimples. When her face would break out she would pick the pimples, and it caused scarring. I recall my grandmother nagging my mother to go to Detroit and have her face sandpapered to smooth her complexion out. My mother always balked at that request.

Interestingly, I recall Mom picking at her face, but I never thought much about it. It's amazing how we condition ourselves and accept bad habits as being normal. For instance, I thought it was normal for families to go out for a drive at night while their Mom and Dad drank a six-pack of beer. What upset me was that very rarely would they take along pop for the four of us.

The big night of the week for us kids was Saturday. Dad would come home from work after the station closed at 10 p.m. and he would usually bring a bag of potato chips and a six-pack of pop. It was great! Then Dad would take a bath and watch what was left of Saturday night boxing.

Sometimes I would play barber with him. He would scoot the couch out enough so I could get behind him while he sat and watched TV. I combed and fussed with his beautiful black hair for a good half-hour. I combed it this way and that. I'd part it on the side or down the middle. Those evenings I played barber will always be a fond memory for me.

Sadly, my mother and father had significant marital problems. I believe my mother suffered from what today we call manic depression. Her ups and downs were monumental. I remember most the depressed states. My mother had a great sense of humor and enjoyed having a good time. However, if she was drinking too much or in a depressed mood, she made life miserable for everyone around her. Her irrational moments were horrible. One time, when Matt and I were watching TV, she became angry with me and insisted we leave. I defiantly said, "No, we're staying put."

"Come on Ellie, let's go," Matt said.

To drive me out of the house she went to the fuse box and pulled the master switch so there was no power in the house at all. We left.

The Gift of Hurt

Another time Mom became angry with me and kicked me out of the house was when I was sixteen or seventeen. I think Dad was angry with me, too, but I cannot remember what I did that warranted being thrown out of the house at 1 a.m. I got in my car, the car my parents bought for me to use as long as I lived at home, and tried to think of a plan of action. I recall being tired and scared, and I did not want to bother any of my relatives or friends because I did not want them to think badly of Mom, Dad, or me. I decided to head toward my grandmother's house, park down the street, and try to get some sleep in the car. When morning broke, I knocked at my grandmother's door and told her I was up early and thought I'd stop in to say hello. I know it sounds lame, but if she didn't buy it, she never told me.

Drinking continued to exacerbate Mom's already precarious mental and physical condition. She slowly became an alcoholic and a hypochondriac. My father seemed oblivious to her drinking, most likely because he was hitting the hooch, too.

Dad was kind but not compassionate. He could be classified as a stoic man who expected the people around him to be stoic, too. Sadly, when you're suffering from a chemical imbalance, as I believe my mother was, understanding and compassion could have gone a long way in reducing the effects and the pain of her disorder. Psychiatric help was not an option back then. People did not go to therapists, they handled their own problems—or mishandled and toughed them out.

To complicate matters, my maternal grandmother was a very strong-willed individual and tried to control my parents. She was tall and had beautiful white hair. She had an almost regal presence, and when entering a room she commanded respect and received it. She was well read although not well educated. Her business acumen was quite sharp. Actually, it probably was because of my grandmother, not my easygoing, good-ol'-boy grandfather, that the family business was successful.

My grandmother was influential in certain areas of town and was well known and well respected for her community service and volunteer work. Facades were very important to her, and she fed that image by hiring a housekeeper named Thelma and employing a bookkeeper for the business by the name of Doris.

I liked Thelma and Doris a lot. I remember Thelma had one leg that was shorter than the other, so she walked with an up and down, up and down gait. Thelma's daughter Marly, who was my mother's age, became one of Mom's closest and lifelong friends. Marly was a pretty lady, but what I most remember was her kindness and sweetness. She married a man named Harold who was a close friend of my father. Harold was a very nice man. He was short and stocky. The four of them maintained a close relationship all through their lives.

Harold and Marly had three children, two daughters and a son. The youngest daughter, Becky, was born mentally retarded. Becky was around my age, though

I believe she had the mentality of an eight-year-old. When Harold and Marly visited our home or when we did anything with them I was coupled with Becky. She was a nice girl but was subjected to ridicule by outsiders. One time we met Harold and Marly at a local church festival. There was polka music, delicious barbecue beef, and kielbasa sandwiches. Becky followed me around, and when we stopped to get something to eat, she was ridiculed by a couple of teenage girls. I could hardly bear their heartless attitude, and though I only gave them a dirty look, it allowed me to gain some insight and compassion toward the mentally retarded.

As I said earlier, my maternal grandfather was a good ol' boy and would have preferred fishing to working. I think his easygoing demeanor allowed my grandmother to dominate their relationship. My mother once confided in me that my grandmother had had an abortion. Mom said that when she was eight or nine she remembered a doctor coming to their home and going into the bedroom, where her mother was, and when he came out Mom overheard the doctor telling her father, "No more baby."

In the 1920s my grandfather earned a considerable amount of money by bootlegging White Lightning. He stored much of it in the radiators around his house. It was at that time that my mother first tasted alcohol. Although she was not bottle-fed White Lightning, consuming it at such a young age set the stage for a way of life that would ultimately be her downfall.

As my mother's drinking escalated, my grandmother and my mother's brother, Robert, did nag my mother in the hope of getting her to stop, but to no avail—most likely because they were the source of a lot of my mother's problems. I know my mother always felt inferior next to Robert and his wife, Joanne. Mom considered herself the less favored child.

It was common knowledge that my grandmother did not like my dad and felt that mom married beneath herself. To further aggravate the situation, it was also my grandmother's belief that having four children was a thankless job and too much work for my mother. She never treated us badly, but I think she wanted my mother to be more of a career woman and live up to her potential.

Meanwhile, my Uncle Robert and Aunt Joanne were having difficulty conceiving a child, so they opted to adopt. My grandmother just hated the idea of a non-blood person taking her name, much less horning into the family. My adopted cousin, Eric, was a very sweet person. A couple of years after they adopted Eric, my aunt became pregnant and had a daughter, Terri. Terri is a fine young lady.

Though I did not realize it then, there was considerable animosity between my mom and my uncle and aunt. I believe Mom liked my aunt but felt she was snobby. The snobbiness was manifested because my aunt had an uncle that was a priest and an aunt that was a nun. I have to tell you that I adored Sister Renaldo, my aunt's aunt. She was kind, loving, and the cutest little nun you'd ever want to see.

A tragic turn of events occurred the last part of the summer in the late 1960s when my grandmother was diagnosed with colon cancer. The doctors gave her six-months to live. When I told my dad, he broke down and cried. It surprised me that Dad took the news so hard. His reaction lead me to believe that he had more affection for her than anyone had thought. It was a difficult time for all of us knowing that the coming holidays would be the last we would celebrate with her.

When spring arrived in all its beautiful colors and the green leaves capped all the trees, my dad told me that he wanted to make amends with his mother-in-law before she died. She had been admitted to the hospital and was frail and in pain. He asked me to accompany him to the hospital. I agreed. I did not warn my grandmother or ask for approval because I thought she would not agree to see him. When we arrived at her room, I said, "Good luck Dad I'll wait here for you."

I could see the fear in his face. He hesitantly entered her room.

An hour or so later he came out and was visibly upset. He looked at me and smiled, "She forgave me."

He was pleased and relieved. Ironically, Dad was dead less than a month after their meeting. My grandmother died two months after Dad.

Chapter Ten
THE STEEL PERSONA

Growing up, I never saw my father cry or show much emotion. I viewed him as strong and being able to take anything that life doled out. It was my belief that Dad had this steel persona partly because he was only twelve-years-old when his father died. My father never talked about his dad very much. My aunts told me that my grandfather worked as a switcher on the railroad. He was crushed by the couplers between railroad cars in 1928 and died a few hours after the accident. He was only forty-eight-years old. Rumor had it that his death was not accidental and that a man who was after his job set up the accident.

My grandfather's death forced my grandmother to raise five young children without the aid of any insurance or governmental assistance. The older children in the family had to quit school and start working. There was no time to feel sorry for themselves because all their energy had to be directed toward the family's survival. Perhaps that is why I perceived my aunts and uncles as being so emotionally strong. They always seemed in control of themselves. That was the kind of grown-up I wanted to become.

One example of the stoic nature that my dad's family exuded was when my grandmother died. I thought her children took her death well. Through the years I watched them bury brothers and sisters, and again their strength struck me as being admirable.

From all accounts, my father was very protective of his younger sister, Millie. She was four-years his junior. When I was growing up she and my Uncle Ron were the closest of my aunts and uncles to us. As I stated earlier, many summers we would rent a cottage on the lake for a week with Aunt Millie and Uncle Ron and my cousins Tommy and Billy. It was great fun, but in no time of my life did I feel the effects of being invisible and, worse yet, a girl than that yearly week at the cottage. I loved to fish and water-ski, but so did everyone else and unfortunately everyone else was given preference. I'm not feeling sorry for myself; I'm stating a fact. Nevertheless, I settled for whatever time I could get on the skis. I would often commandeer an old rod and reel and find a place to fish by myself. Threading a worm on a hook, however, was not one of my favorite things to do. Anyway, I learned that if I wanted to fish with Ken and Tommy, I better be able to bait my line and take any fish I caught off the hook.

I found that although there were stipulations to fishing and water-skiing, I was fortunate enough to garner more than my share of attention when it came to ridicule and sexual curiosity from my cousin, Tommy. Actually it was Tommy who explained to me that when boys "jack off" stuff comes from their "dick." He also demonstrated the procedure, firsthand, if you will, and much to my dismay, in the back of a 1958 Plymouth station wagon. It ended when he threw the gooey evidence in my face.

Tommy never did much to help my self-esteem or confidence. He went on to drop out of high school and drop into the world of drugs and drinking. He was a very handsome boy, but sadly the last time I saw him he was a shell of his former self. Billy the older of the two had maintained a respectable lifestyle and married a wonderful woman named Mary Lou. They had three lovely daughters. Even when I was a child, Billy never ridiculed me or sexually molested me. He was handsome and remains handsome into his late fifties.

Chapter Eleven
THE DEADLY REVELATION

The happy times in the 1950s soon started to crumble as I began to witness the downfall of my mother and father. It began when my father purchased from my grandmother one of the service stations my deceased grandfather left her. My Uncle Robert purchased the other service station. The sales of the service stations left my grandmother a well-to-do widow.

Though Mom did the books and errands for the business, she mostly enjoyed fishing, playing bingo, pinball, dancing, pinochle, crossword puzzles, playing solitaire, and most of all drinking. Her drink of choice was a boilermaker, a beer and a shot of whiskey. Dad mostly enjoyed fishing, boating, pinochle, and, like Mom, drinking.

While growing up I would sit in the living room watching TV with Mom and Dad. Mom sat in her favorite chair, and Dad sat at the end of the couch across the room. Sometimes Mom would sit at the opposite end of the couch, and they would rub each others' feet. In the evenings, they would drink beer, and there would be a fifth of whiskey on the floor by Dad. Every so often he would pour a shot glass of whiskey and give it to Mom to drink or he'd wolf it down himself. I thought that was normal behavior. I spent considerable time making playhouses out of empty beer cases. We had that many cases in our home.

On the good days—and they started to become far and few between—I would see Mom and Dad kiss. A couple of times a week they would go fishing on their sixteen-foot Chriscraft. But what I remember most was their arguing. It was vicious. The daily tension in our home could easily compete with the Battle of Iwo Jima. Most of the time, when their arguing began, I would retreat to my bedroom and cover my ears with my hands and hum loudly to try to drown out the yelling and swearing. I only remember one time when my father struck my mother, and when that happened my sister or brother called Uncle Robert to help out. Most of the time it was just verbal.

Between my parents, it was Mom who acted out most. I fed into her little plan by becoming almost hysterical when she said she was dying. She would argue with Dad, and when he ignored her she would direct her dramatics toward me. I believed them completely. One time she collapsed on her bedroom floor, telling me to call the rescue squad. I called them. When I returned to the bedroom and told her what I had done, she became livid with me and told me to call them back and say they were not needed. I did what she demanded.

Another time they were in the middle of arguing, and all my father wanted to do was to drink his beer and watch TV. My mother hollered, "Ellie come here and help me get this TV up to my bedroom."

"Mom it's too big, just go lie down in bed and don't start any trouble, please."

"Ellie, you push while I pull."

Mom was determined to move the TV up to their bedroom so Dad couldn't watch it. The TV was a big, cumbersome console. We had to negotiate the steps leading upstairs, and as I pushed she pulled. We got that TV up to their bedroom and she plugged it in and watched it. I vaguely remember when I went downstairs again, and saw Dad sitting in the living room, sans TV, he had a smirk on his face. Her actions had to not only bewilder but amuse him.

I spent a great deal of my childhood and young teenage years worrying that Mom would die or leave me. Many times when we would misbehave, Mom would threaten to have us taken away. I believed everything she said and never fully overcame the fear of being dragged away by strangers.

My older brother caught on early that Mom's threats were fakes. My older sister handled her own unhappiness by marrying and moving out when she was eighteen. (I have to admit her marriage wasn't mainly for convenience but love. They have been married over forty-years.) Meanwhile, I tried to shield my baby brother, Paul, but that did not take much energy because he seemed to be unaffected by my parents' antics. I think because everyone adored him and showed him quite a bit of attention it lessened the negative impact on him – at least for the first sixteen-years of his life. After age sixteen, all hell broke loose for him.

When we moved into the new brick house in the suburbs, I saw an excitement in my parents that I never had witnessed before. Dad had the lawn sodded and shrubs put in by a nursery. Mom planted a garden and bragged about her dream come true, a new brick home. Things seemed to be going okay. Boy, was I wrong.

What I did not realize until it was too late is that my mother was an alcoholic. My father talked with me about her drinking and said that he did not realize she drank so much whiskey. He said she had been drinking about a fifth a day. I decided that I would take the bull by the horns and make an appointment with my parents' parish priest and ask him to intervene. As luck would have it, I had just left my parents' house and as I drove past their church, their priest was walking back to the rectory from the church. He was wearing his black cassock and one of those funny-looking black hats. He looked very priestly.

I quickly turned the car into the parking lot and approached him. I introduced myself and explained that my parents held priests in great esteem and I thought it would help them if he would go over to their house and speak with them about their drinking.

"You cannot do anything to help them, you have to wait until they hit bottom, then they'll seek help," He said gruffly.

He was dead wrong. I never did forgive him for his callous attitude toward my parents' disease. I thought then that he was a poor excuse for a priest. That belief was reinforced a couple of years later—he was the same parish priest I called when Matt almost died from an aneurysm. My opinion of him was confirmed then.

Unfortunately, we all experience the death of a loved one sooner or later. I experienced it sooner. It started with the death of my maternal grandfather in the early 1950s, my paternal grandmother in the early 1960s, my mother's death in the late 1960s, then my father's death in 1970, culminating with my maternal grandmother's death, also in 1970. My parents' deaths were tragic, needless, and unexpected. My mother's death seemed to impact me the most.

When I received the Sunday afternoon call in March of the late 1960s from my sister telling me that an ambulance had taken Mom to the hospital, my only thought was to get to her as soon as possible. I found out later that Dad had called an ambulance but did not go with her. I was angry because no one went with her. I raced to the hospital. They admitted her, and because her personal physician was out of town they assigned her to another doctor. I remember the hospital was so crowded that my mother was placed in the hall while she waited for a semi-private room to become available. When I saw her she was in excruciating pain and moaning uncontrollably. She had been sedated, but her pain was still unbearable.

After a couple of days, her new doctor told me that she was suffering from a dependency on alcohol as well as pancreatitis. He said that she was out of the woods. I was relieved because she was going to be all right. I asked him if my mother was an alcoholic, and he said laughingly, "Well she has a need for it, so I guess that's what she is."

My mouth dropped open, and I was shocked that he stated the fact so flippantly. He got right to the point. It was also a shock to hear a professional verify what my father had surmised, that Mom was an alcoholic.

I visited her every day. On Thursday afternoon, four days after she was admitted to the hospital, they finally moved her into a ward. I was upset and voiced that anger to the staff because she wanted a semi-private room. It was explained to me that no such rooms were available. They assured me that as soon as a semi-private room became available Mom would be placed there.

While visiting her Thursday afternoon I was pleased when she announced, "When I get out of the hospital I think I'll go to Alcoholics Anonymous."

My spirits were lifted considerably. As usual, I kissed her goodbye and told her I would come up later in the evening to see her.

That evening, when I walked into her room, she was out of it. She did not know me and kept hitting the sheet and blanket that covered her.

"Get them off me, get them off me," she begged.
"Mom, take it easy, there see I got them off of you."
"Please Mom, are you all right, it's me, Ellie."
She kept insisting that I remove the bugs she thought were crawling on her. I tried to talk to her, but she was hallucinating. I tried to calm her down, but she ignored me. I stopped a nurse and asked her what was happening to my mother, since the doctor had said she was out of the woods. The nurse matter-of-factly told me, "She's suffering from DTs."

I later found out that the doctor had decided to stop the intravenous alcohol, which subsequently caused the delirium tremens. I had read about DTs in high school but I always associated them with a drunk—not my mother.

I left the hospital in tears. I did not know what to do. I did not want to go home because at that time we were still living with my in-laws and I did not like it there. Furthermore, on Thursday nights Matt bowled on a league with his co-workers and would not be there to talk with me. I drove to my sister's house and told her what I saw at the hospital. I was looking for some TLC, but instead, my brother-in-law turned on me like some kind of wounded animal. He began to rant and rave that my mother was an alcoholic, so what could I expect.

"She's an alcoholic, what do you expect? I'm not surprised, I saw it coming."

My sister did not say much because he kept rattling on. I left when he finally shut up. If I had any nerve, I would've told him to go to hell and walked out immediately. When I left I drove around to try to gain some measure of composure. I had no choice but to return to my temporary dwelling. In any event, I needed to hold Randy in my arms.

Later that night, I was sleeping when the phone rang. It was my sister telling me to go to the hospital because Mom had taken a turn for the worse. I was the first one to the hospital and raced all the way up to my mother's room on the third floor. She was sleeping. I was so relieved. Her lips were parted just enough to show a little of her pearly white teeth. She was lying there so peacefully—the complete opposite of when I had left her earlier that evening. I stood alongside her bed, only this time the curtains were drawn around her. I said, "Mom, Mom."

She did not answer. Frightened and confused, I went to the nurses station and asked bluntly, "Is my mother dead?"

I pulled no punches went right for the jugular. The nurse said, "Just a minute," and called on the phone to have a supervisor immediately come to three-east. I shouted at her, "Is my mother dead?"

When she still didn't answer me I shouted, louder again, "Are you waiting for a supervisor to tell me my mother is dead?"

The nurse did not say anything.

I ran back to my mother's room and knelt down by the side of her bed. I stared at her for the longest time. Matt was there with me, but no one else came in. I hugged her, kissed her lips, and joined the rest of my family in the hallway and we wept. My mother was forty-eight-years-old.

My grandmother collapsed when she was told that her only daughter was dead. They administered oxygen to her. My Dad just stood there, stunned. He remained in shock for the rest of his life, which lasted only twenty-six months. He never dealt with Mom's death.

In retrospect, we were not given any preparation for mom's death. We cannot fault the hospital for their directness, but we can admonish them because they did not allow us the dignity or the compassion to let us cry in private. We were told in the hallway, which was lined with patient rooms, that one of the most precious people in our lives had died. Surely, there was a room we could have sat in—even the janitor's closet would have been more private than the main hallway.

I found it almost impossible to leave Mom in the hospital all alone. I wanted to stay with her, but of course they wouldn't allow it. Dad opted not to have an autopsy performed on her. He signed the papers for disposition of her body to the Mortuary.

We left the hospital, and I had to go back to my in-laws' home. I remember when Matt told them that my mother died—all they said was, "Oh." I felt very hurt and offended that they could not even get up and come downstairs and talk with Matt and me. I realize it was in the middle of the night, but their care and concern would have gone a long way to help me heal.

Dad decided that he would show Mom for two-and-a-half days in the funeral home. It was an awful time. My sister called her doctor and got all of us on a medication called Librium. I do not know if it worked. I only know that I hurt badly at my loss. My sister kept telling us, "We have to watch out for Dad because he lost his wife, and we only lost our mother." With that mindset, every time I wanted to break down and grieve I conditioned myself to think, *She's only your mother, think about what poor Dad is going through.*

Dad was devastated and in shock during the whole funeral. One afternoon while he was walking into the mortuary, shortly after returning from what he said was lunch, he collapsed. My brother, Ken and I, caught him just before he hit the ground. He was unconscious for a couple of minutes, and he came to before the rescue squad was called. I think it was a combination of the liquor and the Librium that caused his collapse. We found out later that he did not eat his lunch, he drank it.

Normally, guests are asked to pay their last respects to the deceased first. The immediate family, as a courtesy, are the last ones to bid their loved one goodbye and that is done in private. This mortician had Dad, my grandmother, uncle, brothers, sister, and me say goodbye to Mom first. The mortuary was packed. There were people standing all over and even extending outside. The mortician approached us and gestured for us to say our good-byes. I unsteadily stood up, with Matt's help and looked to my left. I saw a massive number of people staring at us. I cannot remember what Dad, grandma, or my sibs did when they said goodbye to Mom.

When I stood overlooking my beautiful mother in her coffin, I leaned over and ever so gently stroked her beautiful hair, hair so young that it barely breathed with gray. I remember how opposite her hair felt from the rest of her, which was cold and hard. I put my arms around her and held her close to me, so close that we became one. I prayed that the life in me would somehow enter her body and magically make her alive again. I could not bear the thought of leaving her all alone, forever encased in a box, buried deep in the hard dirt, to be left to rot like some animal carcass alongside the road. I found it impossible to let her go, but I knew people were gawking and I had to be stoic. So I kissed her one final time and left.

Dad only lived a couple of years after Mom's death. I never realized my dad loved her so much—it's too bad I did not see it when they were both alive or, more importantly, while I was growing up.

After my mother's death, Dad tried dating a couple of women, but nothing ever came of it. I think they were more drinking pals and a quick lay than anything meaningful and serious. His drinking escalated, and he would not listen to any of us when we asked him to quit.

The man who never cried and who had projected a persona of steel in my youth was slowly destroying himself right before my eyes. All I could do was stand by helplessly and watch him do it. Most mornings his car would be parked outside the local bar—he was more than likely starting the day off with a boilermaker. Sometimes after leaving the bar he would visit me or some other member of my family and drink more.

When Dad visited my home, first thing in the morning, he'd ask for a shot of whiskey and told me to pour it into a water glass. I obeyed him like some type of unfeeling robot and watched as he drank the whiskey from the shaking water glass. After two shots he was as steady as a surgeon. I finally reached the point where I told him that I would not give him anymore booze. He said he would bring his own.

During his visits, he would cry and cry about how much he missed Mom. When I gave birth to my daughter and named her after Mom, he cried more. It really touched him. Shortly after my mother died, Dad stopped working and managing the service station. He left the managing up to my two brothers, who were also trying to deal with Mom's death and were totally unprepared to assume the responsibilities for the station. Every day or so Dad would stop at the station long enough to take money out of the cash register, leave an IOU, and then be on his way. While the business was slowly going down the tubes, with taxes going unpaid, Dad was at the local bar buying all the leeches drinks. He always carried a wad of money. At first glance you would think it was a Michigan bank roll, the kind of money wad that looks like a lot but in reality is made up of $1 bills. However, dad's $1 bills soon gave way to massive numbers of twenties underneath.

Most of the station's regular customers had moved out to the suburbs or other areas of town, and nothing my brothers did could salvage the once prosperous business. To make matters worse, the insurance company canceled the insurance because of the station's high-risk area. John's Sohio was just about dead.

Dad started to get into trouble with the IRS because he did not fill out the forms or pay taxes on the business or pay the employees' Social Security taxes. My brothers tried to do what they could, but they were not knowledgeable about that facet of the business. Mom had always taken care of the paperwork.

In the summer of late 1960 Dad asked me to recommend a doctor for him. He was starting to suffer from tremendous pain in his stomach. I made an appointment for him with my family doctor. During a consultation, the doctor told all of us, "If your Dad continues drinking he will be dead in a year. His liver is severely damaged and needs to repair itself."

He said that if Dad continued on his present path he would destroy what was left of it.

It was difficult for Dad while he went through withdrawal in the hospital. Thank God, his doctor was sensitive and knowledgeable about alcoholism and treated him with medication versus the cold-turkey method that had been used on Mom. He suffered with the shakes and nausea but dried out and was released from the hospital with no mention of seeing a therapist. Even if that had been suggested, he would not have gone. He began drinking tomato juice by the gallon and smoked tons of Lucky Strike cigarettes. Most of the summer he stayed sober, but at the beginning of autumn, he had a relapse and began drinking again.

About eight-months later, my youngest brother, Paul, came racing over to our house and said that Ken had told him to come over and call an ambulance for Dad. Dad's phone had been disconnected for non-payment. Paul said that Dad had fallen and was lying on the floor by his bed, and there was blood all over the place. I returned with Paul to the house. When I walked in Dad's bedroom, he was still struggling to get back into bed. Dad, the floor, and the bedding were soaked in blood. The affects of the alcoholism had made his skin so thin that the constant rubbing as he tried to get back into bed caused his skin to break open.

We helped him into bed, and I told him that an ambulance had been called. Dad begged, "Ellie, don't let me go alone, please ride with me."

"Don't worry Dad I'll stay right with you."

Ken and Paul said they would meet us at the hospital. I assured him that I would not leave him alone. When the ambulance arrived the attendants placed him in the back and asked if I wanted them to turn the siren and the emergency lights on and rush to the hospital. It may sound callous, but by this time rushing was not necessary.

"No, just get to the hospital ASAP, but using the siren and emergency lights were not necessary."

I climbed into the front seat, and we left for the hospital. It seemed like a ride that took hours, but in reality it could not have been more than thirty or forty minutes. I tried talking to Dad, "Everything is going to be OK, Dad. I'm not leaving you."

During the trip to the hospital, the strangest feeling engulfed me when I turned my head to the right and saw Dad's service station. I was unaware that this would be the last time he would go past John's Sohio.

When we arrived at the hospital, my sister and brother-in-law were there. Julie immediately started to chastise me for trying to be a big shot by riding in the ambulance. I just let her ream me out and then went into the emergency room to be with Dad. Of course they admitted him and I stayed until evening and then went home. Paul went home with me.

About 1 a.m. I received a call from the hospital saying that Dad had taken a turn for the worse. I woke Matt and Paul, called Ken and Julie, and asked one of the neighbors to watch my children as we rushed to the hospital. I held Paul's hand all the way there and told him that Dad was probably not going to make it. When we got up to Dad's room, a nurse met us and told us, "Your father has expired."

He died from cirrhosis of the liver. He was fifty-four-years-old. We opted not to have an autopsy performed. Julie signed the papers for disposition of Dad's body and had them call the funeral home.

Dad's last request was to be buried out of the same funeral home as Mom. It seems the owner of the mortuary traded at the service station. In essence, it was all business.

My feelings regarding the mortician had not changed since my mother's death. I still found him to be uncaring, unsympathetic, and lacking in dignity. I remembered after Mom died I related to him that the hospital wanted to perform an autopsy on Mom, but Dad had said no. He said he was glad because, "Autopsies make a mess out of the people. As it was, by the time I got your mother she was already turning black."

He might as well of hit me in the stomach because it damn near made me vomit. I could have easily done without knowing that bit of information.

Immediately after my father was buried, I took a rose from one of his floral arrangements and visited my grandmother. Her favorite flower was the rose. She was unable to attend the funeral because she was in the end stages of cancer. She was living with her son and daughter-in-law, my Uncle Robert and Aunt Joanne. I remember walking into the immaculate kitchen where she was sitting at the table, dressed in her robe. I knelt down in front of her, gave her the rose, put my head on her lap, and sobbed. I felt her stroke my hair, and I remember how much I loved her and how I needed her comforting caress. Eight weeks later I was standing alongside her hospital bed, reciting the Hail Mary, when she died. When I hear someone say that death can be beautiful, I think of my grandmother's death. Her mental and physical sufferings were finally over, and she could see the Lord as He really is. My parents and grandparents are buried in the same cemetery—Calverton—the same cemetery I frequented with my friend Kathy when we were children.

The passing of my father rang the final death knell for the service station. Since he let the house and business insurance lapse, his estate was bankrupt. We did not even have enough money to pay for his funeral expenses. Fortunately, the funeral director gave us time to pay. My brothers assumed responsibility for the funeral bill. With help from Uncle Robert, the bill was paid. My sister and I bought my father's headstone. Thank God Dad paid for his cemetery plot, which was located next to Mom. It was a tragic ending to the lives of two good people who simply lacked parenting skills.

Chapter Twelve

AN ALMOST DEADLY TURN OF FATE

    The next few years I concentrated on raising my children and trying to be a good wife to Matt. I did not realize it then, but I was suffering from depression. I once went to a counselor, though I could not afford it. When he started ragging on my parents I could not handle it and I quit going. To try to find some good out of my parents' death from alcoholism, I became a facilitator for an Alateen group. Alateen is a group for children of alcoholics. They are a spin-off of Alcoholics Anonymous and Ala-anon. There were about a dozen young people in my group. Their ages ranged from twelve to sixteen-years-old and included both boys and girls. At first, they spent a great deal of time testing me, but I was prepared for their inquisition—I had been one of them. At one of the first meetings a girl asked me what gave me the right to facilitate their meeting. She asked, "How do you know what we go through?" I told her in no uncertain terms that I had earned my place as facilitator because I had buried both of my parents because of alcoholism. That shut everyone up, and I was never questioned again.

    I tried to show them that they could count on me for a certain amount of structure and consistency. I gave out my home phone number and gave them permission to call me if they needed to talk with me. They were very troubled individuals to which I could relate and identify. They sought acceptance, trust, love, and for a while I think that's what we had. But, as is the way with the remnants of alcoholism, peace and trust within our group was not long-lived. Bickering and backstabbing started taking its toll. Accusations of homosexual behavior started to spring up, too.

    I wanted to help them very much, but I began receiving late-night telephone calls where one kid would say something about the other kid, and it was becoming increasingly difficult for me to remain impartial. The last straw came when one of the members asked me if I was having an affair with a sixteen-year-old male member. I decided to resign from the program.

    In retrospect, I realized I was in way over my head. I did not have the skills or education to deal with these troubled children. I wanted to help them, but I did not know how to handle the homosexuality or promiscuity among the members of the group. Furthermore, I was upset and concerned about the rumor of me seducing one of the members. I realized the legal implications as well as the moral ones.

    In spite of my short tenure with Alateen, I managed to live a semi-normal life, although Matt's precarious employment became a constant source of insecurity for me. He had worked for a national distribution company for over seven-years and was terminated when they reorganized. He started a new career in trucking, and over the course of twenty-five-years worked on and off in the operations area of that industry. He had worked in the private fleets of a couple of prestigious companies. That employment only lasted three or four years for each, and then they did away with their fleets. Frustrated, heartsick, and insecure, he said that the trucking industry could take their jobs and shove them. At forty-six-years-old he courageously entered into a new career he hoped would be secure and prosperous—selling new luxury cars. He figured if he were going to be selling cars he'd sell the best—the top of the line. What he did not figure on was that his decision would cause such trauma to our family.

Six months into his tenure as a new car salesman was the period in our lives when we were about to gain insight into what was really important in life. The reason for this awakening was Matt's kidnapping. Material things, though nice, mean little if there is no one to share them with you. Job security, also nice to have, means little if you deny your family your presence. What instantly became paramount in our lives were our children and our extended family.

The ramifications of the kidnapping caused Matt mental anguish in flashbacks and fears. He was not coping well and sought therapy, but to no avail. The therapy did not seem to be working. His drinking became uncontrollable, and one night around midnight he was arrested for driving while intoxicated.

Though the judge could have hit him with a large fine and jail time, after being informed of the recent kidnapping, the judge compassionately sent Matt to a weekend rehabilitation program for DWI offenders. He was given the minimum fine and required to enter an alcohol awareness program before his driving privileges were reinstated. When he was sentenced the judge said, "I wish you good luck, sir." That compassionate act and the rehabilitation weekend and counseling for alcohol abuse seemed to be an effective wake-up call for Matt. Since then, Matt has continued to control his drinking.

Matt continued to struggle job-wise and reluctantly decided to return to what he knew best—trucking. In 1997 he was hired to do the bookkeeping and drivers logs for a gutter supply company in their traffic division. He learned Lotus and Excel, and each day his keyboarding skills became better. He said he is happy, although his pay is somewhat low.

PART III

Pamela Crabtree

Chapter Thirteen
BELOVED NEMESIS

One of the many ripple effects that the kidnapping caused—and one that caught us completely off guard—was my almost deadly experience with psychotherapy. Psychotherapy is supposed to be an opportunity to express oneself in a safe and secure environment. The human mind is a complicated and unpredictable machine. A giant misconception many psychologists and their cohorts suffer from is thinking that their education and experience qualifies them to know all there is to know about the human mind and its workings. That attitude is a disservice to those of us who seek their help. It should not be a given that every person responds favorably to psychotherapy.

Like a child playing with matches and getting burned, I discovered that what happened in my childhood should have stayed there. The damage that psychotherapy caused far outweighed any good it elicited. I once heard Dr. Laura Schlessinger of the popular radio show proclaim, "We all are damaged." She was correct. I could have easily lived a full, loving life in spite of the abuses I suffered as a child. What separates the abused is the degree of damage we suffer. Some of us will die with first-degree damage, the rest with second and third degree damage.

During the period I was exposed to my psychotherapists, Ann and Dr. Smith, I found that my personal growth was neither subtle nor slow—it screamed with pain, passion, loyalty, and love.

On the up side, it was an immediate awakening of my potential and capabilities. On the down side, it proved to be the most volatile time of my life—I was like a stream of gasoline heading toward a lit match.

During my tenure with Ann and Dr. Smith I first heard the word *intelligent* used to describe me. It also was the first time I had been exposed to nurturing. Nurturing in its purest form means to be "cared for." It was a feeling as uncomfortable to me as that starched dress I was forced to wear as a child.

From the moment psychotherapy began with Ann, she asked me to call her by her first name. She said, "Thank you" when I asked her to call me Ellie. When the transition from Ann to Dr. Smith occurred, less than a year later, Dr. Smith also asked me to call her by her first name—Barb. She said, "Everyone calls me Barb." I thought, *I am not everyone, and I sure as hell will not refer to another psychologist informally.* The reason for my resistance was simple; I was terrified that I would form the same deep attachment to Dr. Smith as I had with Ann. The pain of termination—abandonment, if you will—was still too fresh in my mind, but more so in my heart. I was not about to risk another rejection.

When I met Ann in the early 1990s I was still struggling with the ramifications of the kidnapping. I had trouble sleeping and a fear of being attacked. I was hypervigilant, and I spooked easily. Even common tasks like doing dishes or dusting my furniture were difficult to complete. It was as if my energy level was drained. Going to the supermarket and putting groceries in the trunk was a regular reminder of what it must feel like to be stuffed into the trunk of a car. It triggered flashbacks of the evening of Matt's kidnapping.

Matt was struggling, too, and I watched helplessly as he battled bouts of restless sleeping. Shortly after the kidnapping he began to jerk while asleep. It would not wake him, but it was a body movement I never saw him exhibit before. He developed an abnormal attachment to me and would not allow me to go anywhere without him. If I did visit someone, I would call the moment I arrived and again when I left.

Matt trusted no one and was angry. Much of his anger was directed toward me for no reason at all. He simply blew things out of proportion. One time I was talking on the phone and he walked into the room. I did not immediately hang up to be with him, and that made him livid. He screamed at me and stomped off into our bedroom. Not sixty seconds later he came out and was kind and loving as though nothing happened.

At my encouragement, Matt started psychotherapy. The doctor quickly diagnosed Matt as suffering from post traumatic stress disorder (PTSD). A couple of weeks later, a friend said to me, "You really need to see someone to help you come to terms with the kidnapping."

Not knowing anyone in the mental health field, I started treatment with Matt's psychotherapist. After a few months under his care, I was at a stalemate. I said to Matt, "I don't seem to be getting any better."

"Me either, therapy doesn't seem to be helping."

We classified our therapist as a "cold fish." His method of therapy did not seem to be conducive to our healing. He used the discipline in therapy of not showing any emotion—I think it is called the blank look. Hell, maybe it was not a blank look at all; maybe that was his personality. I stopped going to him, although Matt continued to see him weekly.

In mid-1993 my life changed drastically as I drove to work. While fiddling with the radio dial, I became intrigued by an interview on one of the local radio stations. The interviewee was a professor from a university. He was seeking volunteers for a research study and therapy program on PTSD. To enter the study, the participant had to have experienced a trauma in his or her life. My thoughts shifted to Matt.

When I arrived at my office I immediately called the professor and left a message on his voicemail. A day or so later he returned my call, and I told him about Matt. He asked me a lot of questions about the kidnapping and said, "Because your husband is in therapy, we can't include him in the program."

The professor explained that mixing therapies could be detrimental to Matt. Then he asked, "What about you? Do you suffer from PTSD?"

"I'm not the victim of the crime."

"Ah, but you are."

He explained that family members can suffer as much as the victim.

"Would you be willing to be screened and tested to see if you suffer from PTSD?"

"Yes."

Two-weeks later I was in the university psychology clinic undergoing testing, screening, and an interview. A few days later the professor called and told me that I indeed suffered from PTSD. He asked me to enter the program. I reluctantly agreed to be a participant.

I was assigned to a graduate student therapist named Ann. She introduced herself when she called my home one evening to set up an appointment with her. She proceeded to explain how the program would work. There would be a total of sixteen therapy sessions. The first eight weeks Ann and I would meet once a week for approximately an hour-and-a-half. Midway, I would be interviewed by another graduate student and asked additional questions. The final part would entail eight more sessions with Ann and then an ending interview.

Ann and I would usually meet in a small room that was equipped with a video camera and tape recorder. We sat on uncomfortable padded chairs with wooden armrests. Ann sat close to me, maybe an arm's length away. The room's decor consisted of a fake wooden bookshelf and a couple of tacky pictures mounted on cement-block walls.

Sometimes we would meet in a larger room. That room was decorated a tad more attractively. Unfortunately, it was located next to the men's restroom, and you could hear whenever the person pulled toilet paper off the dispenser. It was not only embarrassing but a mood breaker.

Our first session began when Ann asked questions about the kidnapping. My answers and reactions were taped on video and audio. I told her early on that I felt ridiculous, especially when she taught me to do some relaxation exercises.

Some of the questions she posed upset me, like how I felt when I found out Matt had been kidnapped. One time after answering one of her many questions, I insolently said, "You remind me of the character on *Saturday Night Live*—you know the one about affirmation— it's okay to feel this way or that way." I don't think she liked to hear that comparison, although she remained passive about my demeaning comment.

She seemed to exude a caring sincerity regarding the kidnapping and said, "It must have been horrible for you while Matt was missing." Showing such compassion made me believe that she was a sympathetic woman—perhaps too sympathetic for her chosen profession.

At one of the first sessions I asked to see her credentials. I did not want a neophyte screwing me up even worse. She said, "I am a doctoral student and have worked for years in the mental health field and counseled Vietnam vets who suffered from PTSD." I thought, *okay, she's competent and well educated.* After prodding her several times to tell me how old she was, she trusted me enough to say, "forty-one." Good, she was not a kid.

The first few sessions were uneventful and centered on establishing a therapeutic alliance and talking about the kidnapping. I would meet her right after work on Tuesday evenings from 5 to 6:30. Afterward I would fill out a form to rate from one to ten how I felt about the session. In the beginning I wrote that I was not getting much from the sessions and that the therapist was ineffective. It did not bother me too much to be ragging on her because I was supposed to reveal what I was feeling after the session.

I gallantly resisted Ann's efforts to form any alliance whatsoever. I maintained a comfortable distance from her and tried not to reveal too much. I felt very cavalier because I was in a research program to help humankind. Most of the time I felt ridiculous and thought Ann was a joke.

However, halfway into the program, I surprisingly found myself becoming closer to this woman. I could tell there was progress in my therapy when I began to respond to a couple of her homework assignments—practicing the relaxation exercises and imagery. Imagery is thinking of something pleasant whenever I thought about the kidnapping.

Ann seemed to offer me her complete and unconditional trust and compassion, no strings attached—a bond between two women. I seized that opportunity cautiously and surprisingly reveled in it.

She accepted me as is; I did not have to play games with her. She conveyed a caring, protective attitude toward me. I felt safe with her, as if she had become my shield from harm. She helped me experience new feelings without stripping away my dignity.

A few months into the research study, strange things began happening to me mentally. As a secretary at an educational institution, I interacted with many of the students. I really enjoyed that contact until one time, while sitting at my desk, a student asked me a question. I looked up, and saw the face of one of my childhood abusers reflected in her glasses. I jerked back, rubbed my eyes, and when I looked up again the image was gone. It left me confused and frightened. I did not connect the psychotherapy with these flashbacks at all.

I made a concerted effort to put all thoughts of my abusive childhood out of my mind. I mistakenly thought that a drink in the evening might calm me down and help me forget. In the beginning, a drink did help me keep my past in check. But as time went on, it seemed to take more alcohol to help me forget. Though I rarely drank before the kidnapping, I became dependent on three or four drinks an evening. My goal was twofold: To diminish the thoughts of my childhood sexual abuse and to diminish the attachment that I had started to form with Ann.

Nevertheless, the flashbacks began occurring more frequently. One time, while in the grocery store, I saw the image of one of my abusers reflected in a showcase glass. I panicked and ran out leaving the grocery-filled cart sitting in the middle of the aisle. The images even occurred when I drove my car and looked into the rearview mirror.

My whole life was being turned upside down as the details of abuses permeated my whole being, twenty-four-hours-a-day, like a growing cancer. Reliving the acts of my childhood sufferings reminded me that I was powerless, alone, and not worthy of protection or love. I expended a great deal of energy believing that I was only good for sex and that I really did not matter to anyone.

While struggling to complete a class at the university, I did research on adult survivors of childhood sexual abuse. Here are some of the findings: The child victim may become an abuser and does not trust. He or she may face a lifelong battle with feelings of worthlessness. Additionally, the child may suffer from low self-esteem, numbness in physical and emotional feelings, and the inability to be intimate with people and enjoy sex. Many adult survivors are determined to leave the pain and ugliness behind, but the scarring never healed properly. Though I was not an abuser myself, I found that many of the other residual affects were quite descriptive of me. I soon discovered that healing was not about the pain, it was about learning to love and respect yourself.

My healing process was inadvertently helped along when I received a long-distance telephone call one-day. On a fateful Wednesday afternoon in March a man called and asked, "Are you missing a class ring?" I was speechless. Of course we were missing a class ring—Matt's ring that was stolen during the kidnapping, now more than two-years-ago. The man said that while he was walking in a downtown Midwest City a bum approached him in need of money and offered to sell the ring for $5. He said it looked like a nice ring, and he thought it might mean something to somebody, so he gave him the money. The man said, "I saw Mr. Jameson's name and school engraved in it and tracked your phone number through the local phone book."

I listened and tried to speak, but I could only cry. I gave the phone to Matt. At the end of the call the man told Matt that he would mail the ring in a few days. We were excited and astounded about the return of the ring.

Several weeks passed and Matt still had not received his ring. The only clue we had to the mystery of the whereabouts of the ring was the man's name and phone number. I called his phone number and received a recording that said the number had been disconnected. In my quest to find the mystery man, I called a reporter with a local paper and explained what had transpired. He said he would write a piece in the paper, and hopefully the man would see it and contact him. After the piece was published, we still heard nothing from the mystery man.

I started to entertain the thought that maybe the whole ring thing was a scam. Was it Matt's kidnapper calling from prison to torture us? Or perhaps he had conned one of his cronies into taunting us. Getting our hopes up was a cruel thing to do—but one hell of a payback after pressing charges against him.

The reporter from the paper called back and said, "Let me do some research and find out where the mystery man lives. I'll go there in-person."

" Great, thank you, we sure would like to get the ring back."

He found the man's address, but when he knocked at the door no one answered. The reporter went there a couple of times, once very early in the morning and then later that night. He waited to see who entered the house. No one entered, although there was a light on inside. He went so far as to leave a note at the house. A couple of days later he received a call from the mystery man. The reporter said, "The Jamesons' have been waiting anxiously for the return of the ring."

"I figured they were. I'll call them right away and explain why I didn't return the ring."

The story he initially told us about being offered the ring by a bum was a lie. In truth, the mystery man was a worker for the Juvenile Corrections Department. He said that while transporting a young offender from our area to a regional juvenile detention facility, as routine policy the prisoner was ordered to empty his pockets. The man saw an expensive ring among the boy's belongings. Recognizing it as a class ring, he quizzed the boy. The boy said someone gave it to him. The corrections officer said, "If you give me the ring, I'll buy you a burger and fries." The boy gave it to him. The officer said that he could get in trouble and possibly lose his job for taking the ring. After his call to us, he became scared. Though he said he did not want a reward, once we received the ring, we sent him $35 tucked in a thank-you card.

What angered me about the whole ordeal was that the ring was found 100 or so miles from where we lived. That should never have happened. If the juvenile authorities were doing their job, they should have seen the ring among the boy's possessions and questioned him about how he obtained it. However, it was obvious they did not monitor this boy at all.

For reasons perhaps only known to psychologists, the ring event caused everything to split wide open mentally for Matt and me. The shock of the call was the catalyst that prompted Matt to reveal a lifelong secret to me.

Chapter Fourteen
A SICKENING DISCLOSURE

Matt sat down across from me at the kitchen table, where I was having another drink. Still reeling from the call about his class ring and trying to cope with the flashbacks of my abusers, Matt impatiently blurted out, "I've been watching you beat yourself up for months, about the sexual abuses you suffered when you were a kid. You blame yourself instead of blaming the fucking wrongdoers—the pedophiles and perverts. I never told you this but I was abused, too!"

My head lifted slowly, and I looked into his glistening eyes. We had been through so much in our three decades of marriage—his physical illnesses, my mental illness, his precarious career moves, the struggle to raise our four children in an unstable economy and the kidnapping. Now this heart-breaking revelation—the story of his own childhood sexual abuse, perpetrated by none other than his grandmother Maggie. This disclosure was impossible for me to fathom.

His revelation was not used as a weapon to hurt but as an instrument to help me overcome my own feelings of guilt. However, his disclosure backfired, and I went into a deeper state of despondency. I felt confused and betrayed because I had liked, even loved this woman, this pedophile. To be told Grandma Maggie had intercourse with Matt at least once-a-week for over four years was, to say the least, a sickening disclosure.

Revealing this detestable liaison drove me to seek out all the details about their clandestine meetings. Matt said as an elementary student his grandma would watch his brother and him at lunch time and then after school. Frequently, when all the children were outside playing, Matt and his grandma would have sex. She said that she was sacrificing herself for him because, "Boys have sexual urges and I don't want you to have sex with strange girls and get a disease."

He believed every word, every platitude she spoke, and grew up believing he owed her a debt of gratitude. It was only after he became sexually active with girls his own age that their incestuous encounters waned.

He never told anyone, until me, that he had intercourse with his grandmother. Both of us regretted the day he divulged his secret to me.

Thank God, it was the usual time for my session with Ann. I practically ran into the counseling room and quickly slammed the door. I stood there shaking and angrily said, "My husband's grandmother fucked him. Fucked her own grandson! I don't want this Goddamn session taped."

She agreed. After calming me down, Ann explained that what I was going through sometimes happens to survivors of sexual abuse. During that session, I became so open, like a bloody wound, that I easily confided to her all the garbage that had been happening to me.

When the session ended Ann walked me to the door and said, "Please call me if you need me, you have my home phone number." The only thing I knew for sure was that I could not cope any longer—I wanted peace, at any cost. I wanted out, *now*!

Chapter Fifteen

MY FRIEND THE SHOTGUN

It was a magnificent-looking piece of hardware. Actually, it was quite beautiful with its polished wooden veneer and its slim black barrel. After taking the shotgun out of the case, I familiarized myself with its mechanics. I opened the bolt and saw the empty chamber. I closed it, cocked it, and slowly pulled it close to my cheek. I looked through the sight, aimed at the wall, and ever so slowly pulled the trigger.

I poured myself another drink and remembered that there was a shotgun shell in the top drawer of Matt's bureau. As a sense of relief engulfed my body, I headed for our bedroom. After rummaging through Matt's bureau, I came up empty. I started a search of the house that spanned five rooms and dozens of drawers and cabinets. "There's got to be a shell somewhere in this Goddamn house," I muttered.

In a moment of coherence and what I perceived as a weakness, I thought of Ann and called the Psychology Clinic hoping to find her there. No one answered. I desperately needed to talk with her. In retrospect, that was the first time in my life that I deliberately reached out to someone for help. After admonishing myself for trying to call her, I resumed searching for the shell.

If I could find it, I would be in control of my destiny. I would become my own comforter, my own executioner. Thoughts of my family and friends were as distant as the tiniest star on a clear summer night. After the futile search, the house looked as if it had been ransacked by burglars.

While fixing another drink, I plotted a second plan for the next day. That plan would entail using my lunch hour to purchase shells from the gun store just minutes away from my home. Before buying the shells, however, I stopped at the local bar for a shot of courage. After downing the drink, I drove across the street and nonchalantly entered the gun store. I asked for shotgun shells and was shown many different kinds. I saw a shotgun that looked similar to Matt's and purchased a box of compatible shells. I hid the shells in the glove compartment of my car under some oil receipts.

When the clock struck five, I dashed out of my office and headed home. When I pulled into my driveway, I was relieved because no other cars were there. I would be alone. I grabbed the box of shells, went in the house, and fixed myself a drink. I slipped one of my favorite CDs into the player and listened as Richard Harris sang "McArthur Park." I listened to another selection by Harris that was poignantly titled "In the Final Hours." I picked up the box of shells, shotgun, and my drink and sat on the floor in back of the sofa in the family room.

I opened the chamber of the gun and inserted the first shell. When I inserted the second shell and tried to pull the bolt shut, it would not close. I tried again and again, pushing and pulling, harder each time, but the bolt would not close. I removed the shells and tried inserting them in a different way—still no luck.

"You bought the wrong shells. You fucking idiot," I snarled to myself.

I decided to initiate a final plan. With that plan I would take Matt's shotgun to the gun store and ask the clerk to assist me with the purchase of the correct shells. As an added backup and to prevent a foul-up like the day before, I would con someone into showing me how to load the weapon.

I waited until it was dark and everyone was asleep. I lifted the gun and gently placed it in the trunk of my car. Step one accomplished.

The next day, I left work at lunch, stopped for a couple of drinks of courage, and went across the street to the gun store. I had to play dumb regarding shotguns to convince the salespeople to show me how to load the weapon. I should have received an award for my portrayal of the loving wife purchasing shotgun shells as a present for her husband's birthday. The woman helped me find the correct shells and showed me how to load the gun.

I returned to work with every intention of going home, loading the shotgun, and putting the thin black barrel in my mouth and pulling its half-moon trigger. Again the clock struck five. I raced home, and as I pulled into the driveway I screamed, "Son of a bitch"—my youngest son, Rick, was home. I had not planned on that. I walked into the house and became angrier when I saw him sitting on the couch, watching sports. I fixed myself a drink and waited, hoping he would leave. He did not.

A couple of days after that flirt with suicide, I had an appointment with Ann. I had no intention of mentioning what I had been planning. Midway in the session she astutely inquired, "How have you been doing? Have you ever thought about hurting yourself."

"Yes."

I told her what happened. She calmly asked, "Would you please give me the gun?"

"No!"

"Look me in the eye and promise that before you attempt anything like that again you will call me"

"I promise to call you."

I gave her my word—but only to pacify her.

A few days passed, and I seemed to be doing better. But that was short-lived as the thoughts of destruction and the shotgun once again became foremost in my mind. After waffling between death and survival, I experienced another fleeting period of rationality and became frightened at what I was thinking of doing to myself.

There I was, sitting at my desk at work, feeling like a nutcase. I immediately called Ann at the clinic. This time she was there. Maybe it was knowing that she was so close that allowed me the strength to reach out to her. I said, "Do you still want the gun?"

"Yes, where is it?"

"In my trunk."

"I'll be right there."

A few minutes later we met in a parking lot. I gave her the gun and some pills that I also thought about taking. She placed everything into her trunk, turned to me, and asked, "Are you all right?"

I gave her my knee-jerk response of, "Yes."

Sadly, I was far from being all right. She said, "You are a very brave person." I watched her every move as she entered her car and drove off.

From that moment, things changed significantly as far as therapy was concerned. More importantly, things changed between Ann and me. I became totally dependent on her. I had not been emotionally dependent on anyone since I was seven-years-old and broke the hold of the adult who was forcing me into the bedroom to say goodbye to my dead grandfather.

Because of my precarious mental state, there had been threats or hints that I might recuperate faster if I were put in the safe environment of a hospital. I became paranoid that the men in the white coats would come and take me away. I confided my concern to Ann, and she said that my condition did not warrant a stay in a mental hospital.

I continued to drink excessively, which aggravated my depressed state. I thought Ann was my only ally and that my family and friends did not care about me. My daughter, Beth, was especially impacted by my declining mental state because she worked in a mental health facility and regularly dealt with at-risk individuals. She also had access to the opinions of psychiatrists and psychologists and confided in them about my mental state. She knew I was in trouble.

Though her co-workers were careful not to presume to diagnose me, they were sensitive to Beth's involvement in my unstable condition. To fuel the fire of a volatile situation, Beth said, "If you won't commit yourself to a hospital, I will call the sheriff and have you pink slipped."

Immediately after Beth's threat, I called Ann at home to speak with her, but her answering machine clicked on. I said, "I'm having a difficult time; please call me." It took her less than an hour to respond to my call. I told her about Beth's threat, and for the first time I heard anger in Ann's voice. She said, "If anyone forces you into a hospital, call me right away and I will come and speak up for you and secure your release." What Ann never found out was on that Friday night, I had a razor blade in my hand as I talked with her. Had she handled the situation any differently, even in the slightest way, I would have slit my wrists.

After Ann's call, I felt at peace. I mattered to someone—I mattered to Ann. I should have been up front with her regarding my intense and growing feelings of attachment. I should have said, "I'm unprepared to deal with these emotions." I was hesitant, even frightened, because I thought she would banish me from her life.

I continued to isolate and distance myself from everyone but Ann. As I began to drink more heavily, I also started to lose weight. Thoughts of my own death became all consuming. I began to court death and plan my self-destruction again.

When the PTSD program was completed, I entered into sexual abuse-centered psychotherapy with Ann. We met twice a week, and she encouraged me to call her at home should I need her. She began therapy by asking me to bring pictures of my parents to our sessions. She also asked me to bring in a couple of pictures of myself around the age of nine, the age when I was sexually penetrated by the stranger in the park.

As my obsession for Ann grew, I hoped that if I saw and talked with her frequently my affection would wane. It did not. As my attachment to her grew, so did my efforts to cover it up. I was sure I had a soulmate in Ann—I was going to find out soon that I was dead wrong.

Chapter Sixteen
GOODBYE ANN

Instead of my feelings dissipating for Ann, they became more intense. Because she helped me open my wounds, I was left with the impression that she made some sort of commitment to me and would never leave. With that belief and trust, I prepared to start the long voyage of disclosing the details of my childhood abuses and working them through with her support. We were at a point in treatment where a tremendous amount of positive psychotherapy could be achieved.

Then my world came crashing down and split wide open—Ann left. Her departure devastated me even more than when my parents died or when that stranger penetrated me in the park, or even when Matt disclosed that he was sexually abused by his grandmother. I have never felt such intense, uncontrollable, and continuous pain as that caused by Ann's departure.

My last session with Ann was on a Friday in the mid 1990s. It was a transitional session in that Ann accompanied me and sat in on my first meeting with my new therapist, Dr. Barbara Smith. With Ann's encouragement, I made the decision to try to accept Dr. Smith as my new therapist. But I told Ann, "I do not want to go to another therapist." However, I was in a lot of distress and I needed a buffer to help me overcome my emotional attachment to Ann. I hated meeting Dr. Smith, I hated Dr. Smith. I did not want anyone but Ann. My heart was breaking because I would not see her again and I could not express my hurt—I could not let her see the weakness in me.

During the session, I sat across from Ann and Dr. Smith, but mostly stared at Ann. I was trying to figure out how I could cope with being alone. I wanted to touch Ann and tell her, "Please don't go, oh God, Ann, don't leave me alone. I cannot do it without you."

But, as I did so often, I camouflaged my feelings.

After the session ended, Ann and I spent half-an-hour alone in one of the offices in Dr. Smith's suite. I asked Ann if we could meet for dinner or lunch or something at the end of the 1990s. After five years it would be ethical for Ann to see me out of the confines of the therapeutic relationship. She didn't say no! When we said goodbye, we hugged, and I said, "Thank you." I tried to project a nonchalant demeanor about our parting.

I got in my car and sobbed. I sobbed until there was not a tear left in me—something Ann might have been surprised to know. I wanted her—no, I needed her—to tell me everything was going to be all right and that I would be able to see and talk with her again. I wanted her to comfort me as my grandmother had when my father died. I wanted her to assure me that the pain would go away.

My family, knowing how difficult the last session would be for me, scheduled a dinner at my favorite restaurant. My brothers and sister and their spouses were all there, as was Matt. I arrived at the restaurant late, and they exhibited considerable relief at seeing me. They hugged me, and we talked about how rough it must have been for me to separate from Ann. They never said anything negative about her. The rest of the dinner was full of laughs and fellowship. Nevertheless, I frequently drifted off and thought about what Ann might be doing at that particular minute.

As I think back to that dinner with my sibs and their spouses, I realized how far we had come in conquering our differences, anger and bitterness toward one another. We began to pull together instead of apart as a family. I was to find out in a couple of years that I was wrong.

As a parting gift I gave Ann a book entitled *Soul Mates* by Thomas Moore. A few weeks later I received a nice thank-you card from her. I could not bear to think that that card would be my last contact with her, so I blatantly committed a cardinal sin of psychotherapy - I overstepped boundaries and acted inappropriately. I wrote and asked Ann to meet me at the local park I frequented. I knew she probably would not, but every time I saw a car that looked like hers, my hopes went up.

A few days after sending the note, I received a phone call from her saying that we needed to meet before she left to clarify boundaries. I was elated and relieved, like an addict who knows she will soon get a fix. Make no mistake—being with Ann was my fix.

We met in the Psychology Clinic, and she was firm, even caustic with me regarding contacting her. She said, "Dr. Smith is your therapist now, and I do not feel comfortable having any contact with you."

She bid me a formal goodbye and practically ran off. I caught up with her in the parking lot and like a child looking for approval from her mother, told her that I was going back to school to earn my degree and that I was going to be a grandmother. She smiled and sped off again.

I viewed her departure as rejection, abandonment, and betrayal. As my loneliness, or what I call my homesickness for her, escalated, I wrote to her. When she did not reply, I became determined to see her or hear her voice at any price. My mental illness was causing me to indulge irrational feelings. What was my lifeline had suddenly turned into an instrument that was choking everything from me.

Dr. Smith inadvertently exacerbated the situation when she told me that Ann probably would not return to the area. She explained to me that when a doctoral candidate does his or her internship, they usually stay within a ninety-mile radius of where they interned. In the back of my mind, I needed to hold on to the hope that Ann would come back and practice in our area. Perhaps then we could finish up what we started. Maybe if she came back she could close the massive wounds she had helped open. Sadly, Dr. Smith completely dashed my hope of Ann ever counseling me again. At that point in my sickness, I was not strong enough to handle or accept that possibility.

Chapter Seventeen
THE REUNION

The summer and fall of the mid 1990s was an on-again off-again relationship between Dr. Smith and me. I would go to a session and then not go back for weeks. She would call me in the evening and ask how I was doing and ask me to schedule a session with her. Dr. Smith said more than once that she had made a commitment to help me and she had every intention of honoring that commitment. She told me numerous times that she volunteered to treat me when she was told about my case from her friend who was a psychology professor, one of Ann's supervisors at the university.

I fought Dr. Smith's commitment valiantly with every ounce of energy I had. I thought, *To hell with her, she'd just betray me like Ann did.* I convinced myself that Dr. Smith was my enemy.

I kept reliving the transitional therapy session and her sanguine comment that, "People find me engaging; if you want a cold fish go back to your former therapist." Her conviction that I would find her engaging was a turn-off for me because I mentally filed her in the back of my mind as being cocky, like the men who abused me—they also saw themselves as engaging, at least where I was concerned.

When I started to see Dr. Smith regularly, she explained that I took Ann's act of termination so badly because it was the culmination of all the rejections I had experienced in my life. As I look back now in my sane state of mind, that makes sense. The problem was aggravated further because my efforts to try to contact Ann turned into an obsession. I could not accept the fact that she was finished with me and denied me contact with her in person, through letters, or over the phone.

My mother-in-law, whom I had grown to love in spite of our rocky start almost three decades earlier, suggested that Matt and I take a vacation and visit Kathy, my childhood friend. Matt and I agreed that it might help if we could get away for a while. We planned a two-week vacation out west. Included in that vacation would be my reunion with Kathy. As the reunion became a reality and airline tickets were purchased, the feelings of excitement, curiosity, and anticipation were replaced by emotions of anxiety, hesitation, and fear. Would Kathy and I be able to reestablish our friendship? Would we be compatible? What could we find to talk about for five days? I said to Matt, "Maybe this was not such a good idea. Who needs the extra stress?"

"It is a good idea, Ellie, you need to see Kathy."

He was right, I wanted and needed to see Kathy, though I would not admit it to anyone.

As the time approached, I became curious as to what Kathy looked like now. Was she gray-haired, chubby, wrinkled, perhaps physically worn out over life's everyday labors and sadness? Or was she perky, sophisticated, svelte, and snobby? Perhaps I made a mistake about pursuing our reunion. Maybe I should have left well enough alone and maintained the image of her as the thirteen-year-old that I had enclosed in my memory. My mind swirled with conceptions and misconceptions of my dear friend. I was frightened.

The big day arrived. As Matt and I boarded the plane for British Columbia, all the anticipation overwhelmed me and I realized that finally my dream was coming true—I would see Kathy. I would be able to actually touch her and look into her eyes as we talked, just like when we were children. The reunion was to take place in our hotel room after we freshened up. I was bursting with nervousness and anticipation. Matt made reservations for the three of us in the hotel dining room—a good idea in the event that the reunion fizzled. You can always find something to talk about during dinner—how the food tastes, the weather, children, and so on.

As I paced excitedly in the room, I heard a knock at the door—I knew Kathy was just a few feet away. I cautiously approached the door that separated us, and when I opened it, inches from me was my dear friend. We stared at one another for what seemed to be an eon. Kathy broke the silence by laughingly asking, "May I come in?"

We embraced, and our tears were visible. I introduced Matt to Kathy, and the three of us talked about the drive from Seattle into British Columbia.

On the pretense of going out for a cigarette, Matt was thoughtful enough to leave us alone, before dinner, so we could visit and renew our friendship. We started talking, and I do not believe we stopped the whole time I visited with her. It was as though we picked up where we left off thirty-five-years ago, like we never had been apart. The compatibility that was forced into dormancy for decades was awakened without so much as a jostle. We spoke about our deceased parents and how we had perceived each other's parents. I was surprised to hear that she had had an unhappy childhood. I believed she was equally surprised to hear about my sad childhood. We traded stories about our children and laughed, noticing that we had each named our youngest sons Rick.

When the time for parting again arrived, it was in dramatic contrast to our nonchalant separation as children. This time, we held one another for what was a long time on the outside but too short in our hearts. I said, "Please write," and walked away quickly. Mirroring a scene from the movies, I started to turn to look at her once again, but caught myself and kept on walking as I waved my arm.

After flying out of Seattle, Matt and I flew into Las Vegas and drove up to San Francisco. We returned via the coast, which took us through Los Angeles, where we had lunch at Jerry's, a famous deli on Ventura Boulevard. It was really exciting because I saw Jon Voight, the actor, walking past us. The waiter said, "Famous people frequent Jerry's all of the time. Valerie Harper, of the *Mary Tyler Moore Show* and the *Rhoda* series was here yesterday."

We continued our trek down the coast and stopped in the affluent communities of Carmel, where we had lunch at the Hog's Breath, Clint Eastwood's restaurant, and visited the Hearst Castle in San Simeon.

Upon our return to Las Vegas, we spent a couple of days with my brother Ken and his wife, Grace. It was a wonderful vacation, and for the first time since I met my student-therapist, Ann, I was able to go through a couple of weeks without constantly thinking of her. I was confident that I had conquered my obsession with her.

Chapter Eighteen
REJECTION PERSONIFIED

When Matt and I returned from our vacation, I had a session with Dr. Smith and said, "I would like to write Ann and tell her about my reunion with Kathy."

"I think that's a good idea," Dr. Smith said.

I mailed the letter and waited for a response from Ann. None came. I could not believe that she could just dismiss me. I sent a second letter. The following is what I wrote:

Dear Ann:

I didn't hear from you, so I was unsure as to whether you received my first letter. I pretty much suspected that you did receive my letter and just haven't had a chance to reply or have opted not to have any contact with me. I understand that internships are grueling and that your time is at a premium. I can appreciate time constraints, and I can also appreciate that you may be having difficulty responding to me after my rude boundary crossing.

In my first letter, I wrote that I do think of you now and again, but it was not all consuming and that I had been coming along slowly but surely. Unfortunately, I recently experienced a setback when I started having dreams about you. I'm trying to cope with the dreams, and one way for me to do it is by risking rejection and connecting with you—even if it is one-sided. You are still, in many ways, my lifeline. I refuse to believe that I'm alone out there when I despair. It's just so difficult for me to reach out—humiliating, even.

In the big scheme of things, although I am no better or worse than most people, I am a very unusual individual. (Do I hear a chuckle?) Unfortunately, there are so few people I connect with, that when someone comes along, even a therapist, it is very precious to me and I do not take it lightly.

As I close, I wish that you would consider contacting me. I'd love to talk with you on the phone and fill you in on what's been happening with my education and Matt's progress in the program, [Matt was finally accepted into the PTSD program after he voluntarily terminated therapy with his therapist]. As I said in my first letter, if you are ever in town I would appreciate your visiting one of my sessions with Dr. Smith. She said she wouldn't mind. You know me well enough to know that I would *never bother you unnecessarily, and my intention is not to become your shadow or receive pro bono counseling.*

I hope you're able to have a nice, restful Thanksgiving with your family.

Ellie

A month later I received the following letter from Ann.

Ellie,

I was pleased to hear from your first letter how well things are going for you. I was surprised to receive your letter given you did not know my address and we had agreed to the fact that there would be no correspondence between us. We both agreed during our last meeting that corresponding would not be beneficial to you and your ability to form a successful therapeutic alliance with Dr. Smith. This agreement was for your benefit. Though I appreciated the letter, I think it's only fair to inform you—once again—that this will end my correspondence with you. If you wish to write, that is fine, but I will not be responding to your letters in the future. I am always interested in you and hearing from you, but I do not feel it is in your best interest to respond. I hope things continue to go well for you and you are able to finish the work you started with Dr. Smith. Good luck!

Sincerely,
Ann

The letter was devastatingly bittersweet. When I first saw it sitting in my mailbox I could not open it fast enough. I read it once quickly and then read it again very slowly. I was pleased that she gave me permission to write, even though she would not respond. I was convinced that if she recognized that I was in pain, she would do the humane thing and respond now and again. I could not see the harm in corresponding with her a couple of times a year. Make no mistake, I believe now as I believed then that had she allowed me the trivial deed of limited contact, the next several years of my life would not have been mired in life-ending pursuits.

I allowed Dr. Smith to read the letter. She became angry and said, "What upset me is that Ann had to zing you, and what you do not need is additional rejection from her."

In spite of the letter, I wrote her back:

Ann:

I received your letter and a very Merry Christmas to you, too. Quite a kicker in the stomach. I have to admit that Dr. Carrol [Ann's supervisor in graduate school] *taught you well, but whether you like it or not and whether I like it or not, we can't deny that we have had an impact on one another. Since you left, I have asked nothing of you except for a few lines of correspondence and a little compassion. You have done a fine job of denying me both.*

Yes, I now recall that in the clinic, I went along with your proposal that we not contact one another. You will recall I said that I would do "whatever you wanted." If you would have said, "Jump off the high-level bridge," at that particular moment, I would have done it.

Dr. Smith has been trying to pick up the pieces that your by-the-book stubbornness has created. You have made her endeavor quite a challenge, not to mention what it has done to me. I continue to struggle with my bond with you and will make every attempt at severing it. Do me a favor, Ann, don't benefit me—let my therapist and me decide how harmful hearing from you will be.

At the risk of angering you further, and as I close, I'm finding it almost impossible to accept that the one person I put all my trust in and my life can reject me so casually. Does any of this disturb you at all? How can you erase me from your life when the profession you have chosen to devote yourself includes people like me?

Ellie

I prayed that Ann possessed enough affection for me that she would want to ease the unbearable pain of separation I suffered. I was wrong. What she did possess was massive amounts of righteous indignation toward me. My efforts to gain attention only proved to increase her contempt for me.

Chapter Nineteen
DIGGING AN EVEN DEEPER HOLE

Dr. Smith encouraged me to keep physically and mentally occupied. I was like a child in that if I had too much free time I would get into trouble. With that in mind and for the first time since Matt's kidnapping, I sat in a classroom at the local university. I took a communications course taught by Professor Esther Wilcoxin. I did not recognize it then, but Esther would play an integral role in my survival and recovery.

I struggled not to write to Ann. I tried not to think of her at all. But working at the same educational institution where Ann was a graduate student, was an automatic trigger. Anytime I went anywhere on campus I would think of Ann. Tears would stream down my face when I had to pass the building where my counseling sessions had been held.

Though quitting my job was an option of ridding myself of one of the reminders, I could not lose the security of my employment. After the kidnapping, I had become the breadwinner and the sole support of our family.

As the months went on I found myself digging an even deeper mental hole with every letter that Ann ignored. My dignity and pride were completely stripped away as I begged her to contact me. In desperation, I concocted an insane plan that would force her to talk to me. I would climb a treacherously high bridge, and when the police arrived I would tell them, "I am going to jump off this bridge unless I can talk with Ann Rudge."

I even went so far as to leave work early one afternoon and drive to the bridge. I parked my car in an appliance repair lot at the foot of the bridge and quickly walked to the middle of the half-mile long span. I started to climb up to the peak of the bridge, by holding onto its inch-thick wired supports. It was not too difficult once I negotiated the first metal landing. The support was structured in such a way that it had makeshift steps with thick wired handles. Though difficult to climb, it could be done. However, after several cars slowed and gawked, I shimmied down for fear someone would try to stop me.

Exhausted, I sat on the sidewalk for a couple of hours, hidden from the world by a solid metal barrier overlooking the river. The rippling white caps that crowned the brown muddy water below mesmerized me. When my trance was finally broken, by the startling blare of a car horn, I pulled myself up and, in Tom Sawyerish manner, walked slowly toward my car, slapping the spindled iron fence with my hand.

When I returned home, there was a generic letter from the university encouraging all faculty and staff to attend the summer commencement ceremony.

Since Ann was scheduled to graduate, I took that invitation literally and hoped that this would be my opportunity to see her.

Prompted by Ann's graduation and my escalating madness, I terminated therapy again with Dr. Smith. I hoped Ann would consider taking me back as her patient. I wrote:

Dr. Smith:

I wanted to let you know I will not be at my session. Also, I am holding you to treat this letter as "privileged" communication. You have always treated me with respect and I truly appreciate that. I'm so sorry I cannot connect w/you the way I did w/Ann—such a waste. I know I need something to pull me through, but I really am weary of not knowing what each day will hold for me. I want to be happy again, but I just can't seem to regain my footing in that direction.

If I can get through Ann's graduation unscathed I should be okay. I only wish Ann and my sister, Julie knew that they are my "seven-minute block." [Meaning that when a person considers suicide, there is a seven-minute block during which if he or she can connect with someone during that time the suicide attempt may well be reflected.] *Right now I am fully aware I could very likely do something to make my point, that ignoring me and not speaking to me is pretty much like pulling the trigger. Again, Dr. Smith I'm holding you to treat this letter as "privileged."*

I have talked with my internist, about voluntary committal. It was my idea. I need to know I have an alternative if I should decide to exercise my process of elimination.

Thanks for letting me vent my feelings, and please be assured that there is nothing you purposely did that prompted my discontinuing therapy. I hope you will allow me to return if I make it through the next few weeks.

By the way, Dr. Smith, it is comforting when you call me even though I sound testy. It helps to know I'm special. If going to Ann's graduation is a mistake, maybe some day you can tell her she really screwed up.

Ellie

Chapter Twenty
THE GRADUATION

My main preoccupation was attending Ann's graduation. I wanted to be there when she received her Ph.D. I wanted to see her hooded—hell, who was I kidding, I just wanted to see her.

Again, in my lunacy, I faxed Ann the following letter just before her graduation ceremony:

Dear Ann,

Please don't dismiss this letter, and if you feel you must send it to Dr. Smith, please be aware that I decided to discontinue therapy with her. I have truly tried to open up this past year to her. I have tried to convince myself that it's working, but an incident last night during therapy pretty much helped me decide that I'm not getting anywhere.

I know you think I'm some kind of wacko, but I'm really not. For some reason, you have been destined to be the only person who was able to make me realize that I'm entitled to feel self-worth. I told you things that I still cannot tell anyone else and though it is just a job for you, it is so much more for me.

I'm so sorry if Dr. Smith offended you and vice versa. You both are talented professionals who will do a lot of good in your career. I'm still searching for my niche, but feel writing may be it.

I'm writing because I really need to talk with you. Please don't be afraid of me. I couldn't hurt a fly—I just need to talk with you. Don't punish me any longer, I don't know why I can only connect with you.

Ellie

When I still did not hear from her, it placed another rung in my ladder of madness. I sent another fax to her a couple of days later.

Dear Ann:

I ask— no, I implore you to become my therapist. No matter the cost. I can't go back to Dr. Smith, and please don't humiliate me any longer by making me send faxes for anyone's eyes to see. I am aware that I have put you in an emotionally impossible position and have been a pain in the butt, but if you will not consent to be my therapist, I don't know who I can turn to.

I know one thing for sure; I just cannot go on this way. I have absolutely lost all my dignity, as this fax demonstrates. I also know that I am really messed up. God, Ann, I should never have gotten into the PTSD study. In my case, leaving sleeping dogs lie would have been a good thing.
   Please don't be the lifeline that chokes everything from me!
Ellie

Ann had been sending my mail correspondence back to me via Dr. Smith, but the faxes were being returned to me personally as undeliverable. In spite of her humiliating tactics, because the people I worked with saw the undeliverable faxes, I continued my crusade. As my sickness grew worse, triggered by Ann's ignoring me, I dodged Dr. Smith's attempts at contacting me. She tried again to connect with me and would often use my new grandson as a tool for making my life worth living. In retrospect I know why she drilled into me about turning to my grandson. His giggles helped me through the heartache I experienced from Ann's rejection. He was the only one who could make me feel better. I adored him and loved him desperately; nevertheless, I still wanted to die and stop the hurt from the loss of Ann.

My obsession with Ann mounted, and I continued to reject Dr. Smith's efforts to contact me. I was terrified that if I kept seeing her I would become dependent on her, too.

When Ann's graduation day arrived I was at the site two-hours before commencement. I seated myself right in front of the stage where she would have to walk. I even took a book along to read and clicked my Walkman on so I could listen to some depressing music, like Johnny Mathis's "When Sunny Gets Blue."

I sat there for over two-hours. While fiddling with my Walkman, I looked up and nonchalantly turned to my left. There she was, down on the field, lining up for the processional. Her presence stood out to me like black on red. In spite of knowing that I would see her, when it happened, I was stunned, awestruck. My first emotion was a sense of tranquillity—I had my fix. I felt comforted and knew that while I was so close to her, nothing bad could happen. No one would hurt me, but more important, I would not hurt myself. My eyes did not drift from her for a moment. One time she started to walk toward me and I thought, *Oh son-of-a-bitch, she saw me and is going to tell me to leave.* She walked right past me and went up into the visitors area.

During the commencement, I stared at her whenever I could see her. I tried not to lose sight of her among all the caps that seemed to form a united blanket of black. After the two-hour ceremony, I watched to see which gate she exited, but there were too many people scrambling around and I lost sight of her. What I had intended to do that day was look her in the eye and hoped she would see the sadness and pain in my eyes that she caused and that only she could alleviate.

I had seriously entertained thoughts of taking a gun, and as she was hooded on stage I would run up and shoot myself in the temple. But after some thought, I decided that I did not want to ruin her special day—one that she worked so hard to achieve.

Since I was uncertain about what gate she would exit, I took my chances and waited at one of the recessional gates. While waiting there, I saw Professor Wilcoxin exit. When she spotted me, she came over and hugged me and asked me how I was holding up. I had confided in her that I would be at the graduation in the hope of seeing Ann. Esther was an officer in one of the organizations and sat on stage during commencement, so she got to see Ann up close. In fact, Esther kidded me that when Ann came up, she was going to put her foot out to trip her. We laughed about that, and then Esther went on her way. I continued to stand and wait for Ann, but to no avail. I never saw her again.

Because I controlled myself during the graduation, I rewarded myself by calling Ann's house and leaving a message on her voicemail.

"Now that you're an official doctor, would you please allow me to become your patient again?"

Ann called Dr. Smith—she always called Dr. Smith—and bitched about my call. Nevertheless, my inner madness demanded that I see or talk to Ann or kill myself. Interestingly, though Ann never hesitated to call Dr. Smith to gripe about me, she never took Dr. Smith's suggestions about how to best treat my condition. The treatment, which was never given a chance to succeed or fail, would have been for me to see or talk with Ann. However, instead of working with Dr. Smith to help me overcome my dependency on her, Ann bucked Dr. Smith's every request for help. I found out later that after her graduation and internship Ann did indeed return to our area and started practicing psychotherapy. Dr. Smith had been wrong when she told me more than likely Ann would stay close to her internship area.

Chapter Twenty-One
COME AND GET ME

The peace and comfort generated from seeing Ann at her graduation soon wore off. In my quest to break my obsession with her, I began playing games by putting myself in physical jeopardy. Because I failed at killing myself before, perhaps someone in the criminal sector would do it for me. That way, I would be free from the stigma of suicide and the wrath of God. Additionally, it would lessen the embarrassment to my family.

One evening around 11 p.m., I placed my personal belongings in the trunk of my white Grand Am and drove to one of the most dangerous areas of town, where undesirables walked the streets and preyed on the weak. That action was akin to walking alone in New York's Central Park in the middle of the night. I was emotionally spent, lacked sleep, and was intoxicated when I drove into this drug-laden neighborhood. I parked my car next to a barren cement island that used to be home to gasoline pumps. Across the street was a rundown mom-and-pop grocery store.

I peered to see if anyone was around. I saw no one. I thought, *Too bad for them, I will not put up a struggle.* I stood there, vulnerable, like a wounded animal, waiting. After an hour or so, restlessness set in; I returned to my car and drove away. I tried that trick a couple more times, thinking the more I went there the better the odds of being killed.

Each day I woke with the pain of Ann's rejection and needed booze to help me sleep and work around the inner trauma. Every day I would go to my favorite park and walk or run several miles to try to rid myself of the obsession. One time while running, tears welled up in my eyes and caused everything to become blurred and distorted—as distorted as my life had become. I dropped to my knees and screamed out, "Ann help me." I knelt and sobbed. Luckily, no one came down the isolated path. I regained my composure and started back. Before I left, I eyed an area that was so secluded and unobtrusive that I gave serious thought to taking a razor blade with me on my next jaunt and ending my obsession with Ann.

It came to pass that the rare times I was not concocting ways to eliminate myself I was sitting on the porch of the counseling center where Ann had started working. I would drive there late at night, knowing no one would be there. I would sit, smug with the knowledge that I could be somewhere Ann frequented. I prayed that she would take pity on me and at least let me talk with her. I desperately needed closure.

A few times I would drive past her house late at night. On more than one occasion I fought the temptation to knock on her door and beg her to talk with me. I would settle for her to say, "Go to hell," even spit on me, anything—just an acknowledgment that I existed to her. By driving past Ann's house, it alleviated some of my pain—for that moment I could connect with her. It also helped to fend off that all-consuming desire of driving to the worst part of town and walking the streets.

As my mental state continued to plummet, my dear sister-in-law Grace said, "I'm not going to sit by and watch you self-destruct. You must go back to Dr. Smith."

"Grace, I can't - Grace, I will try to return."

Grace helped me through some difficult moments just by giving me an ear and some of her time. With encouragement from Grace and Dr. Smith's support, I returned to counseling.

At some point in my daily struggle, my disappointment with Ann turned into resentment. It was triggered by an incident that happened at my office. I exhaustedly went to work and when checking my voicemail I was startled when I heard one of the most devastating messages of my life. It was the voice of a young man laughing, with other people laughing in the background, yelling derogatory remarks into the phone accusing me of being a "fucking fag." He cursed and called me horrible names. Thank God the voicemail timer cut him off. I firmly believe that the young man was Ann's son. He would have been around twenty-years-old.

I could not blame him too much. I am sure he intercepted and heard many of the calls I made to Ann at her home. I was not shy about leaving my work and home phone numbers on her machine. He had probably witnessed her frustration and unhappiness with my actions and reacted by verbally attacking me. To add to my already mounting humiliation, Ann informed many professionals about my case and warned secretaries and office managers about me—just in case I would try to contact her.

Chapter Twenty-Two
DR. SMITH, PLEASE HELP ME

When I thought things could not possibly get worse, a nearly fatal situation arose a week before Christmas in the mid 1990s. As usual, I kept my appointment with Dr. Smith. However, as I walked down the stairs to her office, the staff of many of the adjacent offices were having a common Christmas party. They commandeered the huge waiting area outside Dr. Smith's office, and food and presents were strewn all over the area in front of her door. Though there was access to her door, in order to see Dr. Smith, I would have to walk through a crowd of people.

I tried to go down, I really did. I would struggle to go a few steps and then go back up and look down on the party. I would say to myself, "Come on Ellie. Come on Girl, you can do it." "Just keep your eye on Dr. Smith's door. She's right through that door."

I desperately needed to see Dr. Smith, but I could not get to her. I was always embarrassed and humiliated while waiting for Dr. Smith in her waiting room. Knowing so many people would see me enter a psychologist's office was even more disturbing.

"Please Dr. Smith come and get me. If you care about me, Oh God Dr. Smith find me."

I prayed Dr. Smith would come up and try to find me, but she didn't. Subsequently, I figured she did not care about me. I thought, *Ann will not see me, now I cannot see Dr. Smith—I want out—no more fucking around.* These women had holds of steel on me, and it was killing me.

Feeling alone and defeated, I reluctantly went home. I did not have a gun, I did not have pills, and I did not want to fool around with razor blades. Since no one would not be home until much later, I decided to go into my garage, close the door, and run the car until I was out of my misery. I knew that I needed a few drinks to give myself that extra courage to stay in the car. I was already exhausted, so drinking would only prove to make me more tired and if I kept swilling the booze, I would just fall asleep behind the wheel and never know what happened.

I quickly drank a couple of Manhattans, dwelled on the belief that my life was shit, and went into the garage. I got into my car, started the motor, turned the radio to an easy listening station, and took a swig of bourbon. About fifteen minutes later, I felt dizzy. At that point I do not know if it was the carbon monoxide or the booze that was making me dizzy. In time I did not care what was making me woozy, I just felt relieved that my painful life was coming to an end.

A few minutes into my welcome sleep, I was startled awake by the roar of the garage door opening and the shock at the sight of my two sons standing there. Humiliated, I yelled, "Stay the hell away from me."

I staggered into the house, grabbed some money, got back in my car, and sped out of the garage.

I was so upset and drunk that I only wanted to go someplace and drink more to figure out what to do next. I checked into a cheap motel. The clerk asked no questions when I paid cash. I opened the door to my room, turned on the TV, and got ice from the ice machine. I made myself a drink and thought about calling Dr. Smith. Instead, I called Ann. No one answered. I continued drinking and heard a knock at the door. I looked through the peephole and I saw a man in uniform.

"Who is it?"

In a blustery voice he said, "The sheriff."

"Just a minute."

I put my trench coat on because I had taken off my clothes.

When I opened the door, he walked in and asked, "What are you doing?"

"I'm drinking and not bothering anyone."

There were several police cars in front of my door. I also saw a police officer on either side of the door. I guess they must have thought of me as public enemy number one, or else they thought that they were going to find a dead body, "Are you going to hurt yourself?"

"No, I just want to be left alone."

"Why are you so upset."

"I had a difficult time with my therapist and needed to be alone."

He spotted the liquor and said, "If you drink, make sure you stay inside and don't get behind the wheel."

"OK."

He and his entourage left.

I found out that my daughter had called the police after her brothers told her where they had found me. Matt did not want the police involved. To this day Matt cannot talk with me about the times I tried to kill myself. I do not think he ever accepted the depths of my despondency during those terrible years.

When I was not tempting fate with a shotgun or carbon monoxide, I holed up in cruddy motel rooms with a bottle of bourbon and razor blades. I would become so drunk that when I swiped the razor over my wrists, the physical hurt did not outweigh the massive mental anguish I suffered.

One weekend, when Matt hesitantly went out of town to the Football Hall of Fame with our children, I made a game of playing with razor blades. I gathered a few towels and took them in the bedroom, where I proceeded to puncture and cut my wrists in several places. I kept the towels handy so I would not make a bloody mess on the bed. I thought if I would cut them in several places it would increase my chances of hitting a vein and bleeding to death.

I played a game of Russian roulette with a package of razor blades. Though I did not win at the game, I made a terrible mess out of my wrists. I still carry the scars as a reminder of my lunacy. I tried to cover up the cuts by wearing long-sleeved blouses, but Matt spotted my injured wrists and asked me about them.

"I fell while getting wood for the fireplace Matt, no big deal."

He did not buy the excuse and wasted no time notifying Dr. Smith.

In spite of my rebellious attitude and my attempts to kill myself, Dr. Smith did not abandon me and tried to convince me that she would always be there for me. I did not believe her. I knew she would leave me, just like Ann had—it would only be a matter of time.

Chapter Twenty-Three
THE MADNESS ESCALATES

Ann and Dr. Smith's professional relationship had become strained because of me, and I felt responsible. Additionally, I found out that Ann was talking with professors at the university about Dr. Smith and me. With that information, I requested a meeting with those professors to explain Dr. Smith's motive. The sad thing about the situation was that Dr. Smith had formed a personal friendship with one of the professors. The intention of the meeting was twofold. First, I wanted to explain that it was not Dr. Smith's intent or mine to upset Ann or impugn her reputation. Second, they needed to be aware that Dr. Smith was using every means possible to save my life. The professors agreed to meet with me for half-an-hour. When I was escorted into an office the first question out of one professor's mouth was, "Are you going to hurt yourself?"

"No."

I would not have told the son-of-a-bitch the truth anyway. I said, "My termination from Ann was botched, and this mess is not Dr. Smith's fault. She is trying to clean up your botched psychotherapy. I responded normally to Ann's nurturing and it became problematic because I developed a special bond, which turned into a sweet, innocent love from one human being to another."

I finished by telling them that I was going to terminate therapy with Dr. Smith. The meeting ended after I said, "All I want to do is talk with Ann one more time."

In spite of my personal pleas, the situation became completely blown out of proportion as accusations of unethical behavior were directed toward Dr. Smith and whipped around like trees in a hurricane. It must have been extremely difficult and painful for her to take the blows of reproach from peers who made unfounded and unfair allegations regarding her professional ethics. Even so, with all the flak showering down on her, she never stopped voicing her opinion that I had been treated unfairly by Ann.

Dr. Smith and I talked about the accusations on the phone and in my final session with her. Shortly afterward, I received the following letter from Dr. Smith:

Dear Ellie,
    I received your fax and was distressed by your decision and blaming of yourself. I do like you, and I feel like I can help you. I think you have come partway through all of the distress you are feeling about Ann. Life is not fair, and people make mistakes all the time. That is the way life is!

It is trying to decide peoples' intentions as well as trying to protect yourself from harm and hurt yet still remain open that I see as one of the primary goals of living. I have a desire to make things more fair and more caring in the world, and I know I will never succeed 100 percent and that I will do some things that are unfair and make mistakes. Yet overall my intentions are honorable. I also do a pretty good job of taking care of myself—protecting myself from hurt and harm and still remain open. Numerous people have made numerous mistakes in the past six months. As far as I can tell, most of these mistakes have been based on misinformation, and there has not been the intent to hurt. However, that does not mean that hurt has not occurred to you, as we both know it certainly has. And you and I know that you feel that some of your behavior worsened your situation with Ann. You have not had any intention to hurt anyone, in fact quite the opposite. I will leave your appointment time open for you. I will be there waiting for you. After that if I do not hear from you, I will book your appointment time with someone else. I know you asked me not to call you or fax, but you didn't say I couldn't write. See, we therapists can be tricky, too. I will not bother you after this letter unless I feel an urgent need to do so, and I will respect your decision not to see me because I have no choice. As you know, I do not see that decision as in your best interest and I do not see it as in my best interests either. Whatever you decide I wish you well.

Barb a.k.a. Dr. Smith

A day later, I received this letter from Dr. Smith:

Dear Ellie,
   There are a couple more things I need to say. I misjudged things on Thursday night, and I never should have told you what the Department said about me. I should have known that you would judge yourself responsible and should have kept it to myself—I know it will all turn out all right with them anyway. I do not want the cost of my error to be your quitting therapy or killing yourself. I would feel forever guilty. Again, I made a mistake, but my intention was not to harm/hurt. My natural tendency to be very honest coupled with what's going on between myself and my partner left me not in a good space to make good decisions about what to share and what not to share. I underestimated big time—your willingness to blame yourself and your wanting to protect me. If you want to help me, come back to therapy and forgive me my error in judgment—there may be a time when you will ask me to do the same for you—sorry this is hand written—I know I write like a doctor.

Barb

I relented and went back into therapy.

I always pressed Dr. Smith to tell me what transpired whenever anyone talked about me. Once she told me that in a conversation with Ann, Ann had inferred that I sexually desired her. That belief was probably triggered by my admission that I loved her. It continued to hurt me, because Ann viewed my affection as perverted and not the way it truly was—a childlike love for another woman. Nevertheless, it did give me a pause to question my sexual preference. Maybe Ann's son was correct in the vicious insults he and his buddies left on my voicemail?

To twist my fears further, Ann's accusation that I sexually desired her was reinforced by my affection for Dr. Smith as well as the difficulty I was then experiencing in my sex life with Matt.

Though it might not seem possible, the situation grew even worse between Ann and me when Dr. Smith told me that Ann voiced to her that she believed I was litigious. Dr. Smith was becoming fed up with Ann's opinion of me and in anger said to her, "You do not have to worry about Ellie suing you, because if she kills herself, her family will sue you."

After that last confrontation between Dr. Smith and Ann, I felt obliged to write Ann a short note. However, it did not take much for me to find a reason to write her. The note went as follows:

Dear Ann,

Please be assured that I have never had any litigious intentions toward you. On my worst day, suing you never even entered my mind. I thought you knew me better. It disturbs me greatly and is continually on my mind that you are fearful of me. If I weren't so fucking stupid, I'd be angry with you. My only motive in this whole mess is that I wanted to keep in touch with you, to get your attention so that you know I still exist, plain and simple. One phone call to me saying that things really got out of hand regarding my termination and that you weren't sure how to handle it would have helped me so much. Jesus, Ann I know you're a human being and like all of us make mistakes, but to even entertain the thought that I would sue you. I'm so sorry I caused this whole situation. I never wanted you and Dr. Smith at each other's throats. She was just trying to help me the best way she could.

Ellie

Because I bombarded her with correspondence, I think Ann's judgment became distorted where I was concerned, and I think she inadvertently punished me by denying me any contact with her. However, similar to the snowball effect, the more she ignored me the more maniacal I became that I must see her, talk to her, or die. The pain of her rejection was of such a magnitude that over the years it sapped every ounce of dignity, thoughtfulness, and common sense I ever possessed. I was left with nothing—or so I believed.

Not only was my relationship with my family negatively affected, but my association with my co-workers at the university became quite strained. I stopped talking with them and became distant. Most lunch hours were spent at the park, where I would walk and obsess about Ann and figure out ways to rid myself of my dependency on her. Some of my lunch hours were spent drinking.

My irrational feelings became the foundation for bizarre behaviors. Several times during the day or night, I would drive to the cemetery where my parents were buried and park in front of the entrance gate. One night I found an open gate, entered, and went to their graves. I knelt by their headstones and frantically cried and dug at my mother's grave with my fingers. I made a mess out of the grass that covered her grave. I made a mess out of myself, too.

Like two trains on the same track heading uncontrollably toward each other, Ann and Dr. Smith's conflict mounted to the point where they acted completely unprofessionally. They seemed to lose perspective that the one who was being damaged the most because of their bickering was me.

One weekend, when the situation between Ann and Dr. Smith reached a peak, Matt and I spent a couple of days at my brother's condo on the lake. The condo was only fifteen minutes from Ann's office. I told Matt, "I'm going out for a newspaper and a cup of coffee." Instead, I drove to Ann's office, but no one was there. Feelings of guilt began to creep up on me, and I needed her forgiveness. I stopped at the local newspaper office and asked if they would be interested in printing a letter I had written to one of their town's psychologists trying to apologize for any pain I caused her. At first they were interested in my story, but at the last minute they withdrew the piece. I never found out why they decided against printing it. The editor suggested placing it in the personals column. I agreed and wrote: "Dr. Ann, please accept my apology for pursuing you." I signed only my first name.

Chapter Twenty-Four
THE LONG WALK INTO OBLIVION

When Matt and I returned from our weekend, I continued to be upset because of the newspaper's refusal to print my letter to Ann. In one of many impulsive acts, I sped off in my car. At an intersection not far from my home, the car acted up and stalled out. I nursed it to the parking lot of a nearby high school.

There I sat, stranded in a school parking lot and feeling angry at every living thing. I did not know how to defuse the rage. My thoughts turned to Dr. Smith and how I needed to talk with her. I became obsessed with getting to her office. I looked down at my feet and realized that in my haste to leave my home, I had not put my shoes on. I did not let that stop me from running and walking over two miles to her office over stones, hot asphalt, and glass. When I finally arrived, my feet were bloody. There were no sidewalks between the school parking lot and Dr. Smith's office.

The sun was setting, and it was obvious no one was inside the office. I practically collapsed on the front porch and managed to crawl and huddle in a corner. I lay there for some time before a car pulled up. It was Matt. He said, "I have been worried sick about you."

"Just let me stay a half-hour and then I'll go home with you."

"Ok, but only a half-hour. I'll be back."

Oblivious to his concern for me, I was in constant pain because Ann was seeing other patients but would not see me or talk with me. In spite of her requests not to contact her, I continued to write. I wanted an acknowledgment.

Dr. Smith's attitude against Ann and her support for me but not my impulsive actions, lead Dr. Smith and me into uncharted waters when we both received threatening letters. Mine came by certified mail and read:

Ms. Jameson:

I am once again requesting that you refrain from contacting me and/or attempting to contact me either at home, in public, or at my place of employment. If you continue with this behavior, I will be forced to press charges for harassment/stalking. Please respect my request and keep this from proceeding any further.

Ann Rudge, Ph.D.

After reading the letter I cried, like I had frequently cried when it came to Ann. This time I called my supervisor at work, and told her, "I quit."

"Ellie, you cannot quit, the best thing for you to do is to come to work."

"I can't cope anymore and I haven't been stalking or harassing Ann."

"I know, I know, she is not fit to shine your shoes and you must overcome your attachment to her. I will not accept your resignation"

I knew that she was right.

While I struggled with the nasty letter from Ann, Dr. Smith was trying to make some sense out of a formal letter she received from Ann. It stated that if she continued to encourage contact between Ann and me, and if Dr. Smith revealed where Ann was working, she would file charges of unethical behavior against Dr. Smith with the state psychology board.

I had not talked with Ann since the summer of 1994. In addition, she listed her place of employment and her personal residence in the phone book. At this point Dr. Smith believed Ann was becoming paranoid where I was concerned. She told me that she hoped Ann would not accept any patients that might require intense, intimate therapy because Ann was incapable of making a commitment to that patient.

While I struggled with my depression and constant thoughts of ways to kill myself, Matt dropped out of the PTSD program and began seeing a psychologist. They addressed many issues during Matt's therapy, including the kidnapping, sexual abuse, my state of mind, and Matt's own thoughts of suicide. At one point in therapy, I was asked to attend one of Matt's sessions. It did not go well. I was angry, uncooperative, and arrogant. I could see that this therapist was helping Matt, and instead of being pleased I used their relationship in a horribly distorted manner.

Matt knew I was trying to crash and burn and that Dr. Smith was working with me to overcome my despair. One evening after returning home from my session, I told Matt, "Dr. Smith felt that since I am hesitant about killing myself, you should help me by taking the shotgun and shooting me and then kill yourself. That way we will be out of our pain."

Matt was shocked that Dr. Smith would suggest such a sick solution. Nonetheless, I felt I had planted a seed and that if Matt truly loved me and wanted me out of my misery, he would follow through. He was vulnerable and fighting his own battle with depression, and I took unfair advantage of his sickness with this lie.

Instead of acting on the murder/suicide idea, Matt went to his therapist and told him of "Dr. Smith's" suggestion. Matt's doctor was horrified and could not believe that a respected therapist like Dr. Smith would encourage such a notion.

When Matt told me that he mentioned the idea to his doctor, I went into a rage. I cursed him and walked out. I thought, *Jesus Christ, if Matt's doctor calls Smith and they talk, everything I planned would go down the toilet.* I knew I was in trouble and that I had to admit what I had done to Dr. Smith.

At my next session, I told her what I had done. She nearly flipped out. She was visually angry but tried to remain in control. She told me the ramifications that my action could cause her. Among other things, her reputation could become ruined. I felt badly and attempted to rectify my deed. I first apologized to Dr. Smith and then wrote a letter telling Matt's doctor that I had lied. I then apologized to Matt.

Chapter Twenty-Five
THE CONTROVERSIAL DR. SMITH

During my sessions, I found myself sitting across from Dr. Smith, baiting her at every turn. She began to try something a little different in therapy in hopes of helping me. She allowed me to see her own human side, including her imperfections. She would tell me what a bad day she was having or when she suffered a migraine. One time while walking into her office she said, "I am moving, and my phone number is changing." I asked, "Is your husband moving with you?"

She said quietly, "No." We discussed her marital situation a few times, until she told me that she did not want to talk about it any more. Since then, she and her husband of over twenty-years have divorced.

I found myself responding to her disclosures, but I did not want her to know she was getting through to me. I began to imagine that sharing intimate things with me was an indication that our relationship was special—that I was special. Talk about déjà-vu. Nevertheless, she continued to startle me with her personal glimpses. I had met her husband, mother, father, and sister. I knew what her husband did for a living, where he worked, and when she separated from him. I learned many personal things about her, and it completely confused me. Ann would not tell me anything, but Dr. Smith revealed more than what I needed to know.

When I questioned Dr. Smith's forthrightness, she said, "It's what you need," meaning that what I did not need was another therapist who I thought walked on water. I should have basked in the concern and affection that Dr. Smith showed me. Instead, I fought her every step of the way.

During the years I was her patient, she sent me cards when she was on vacation and at times when therapy became very demanding for me. It was no wonder I began to respond to her and hold her in high esteem.

I found it increasingly difficult to turn away from Dr. Smith as she slowly and gently instilled a trust, a small one that allowed me to grab onto her coattail so she could lift me to her and away from Ann. She could see clearly where my vision was obstructed. I found it extremely difficult to let go and allow her to manage things until I was mentally better. I continued to feel trapped and terrified that she would abandon me as Ann had.

In spite of my struggle to distance myself from her, I began to depend on her as much as I had depended on Ann. However, I had to deal with separation anxiety every time I left her. She was understanding, patient, and compassionate and told me, "I bet if you could, you would crawl in my skin with me."

"Dr. Smith, that is exactly how I feel."

I recall one time when she went to Florida for a whole month—I about died. The pain of separation, the loneliness was unbearable. All I did while Dr. Smith was gone was drink and vow to myself that somehow I would get out of this attachment to her. She knew I was in pain, so she gave me her number in Florida. I fought the need to call her. Oh, God, I wanted to, but I did not, mainly because I felt she needed rest away from all her patients, especially me.

During my struggle, my sister decided that it would be the best thing for her if we did not speak anymore. She was trying to cope with the demons that had invaded her own home and obviously could not handle my untenable behavior plus her own problems.

When Dr. Smith returned from Florida she said, "Why don't you call me every day—just to touch base or check in. It might make you feel better."

"I would really like to do that, I want to do that, but I would feel so humiliated."

"How about I call you, Ellie?"

"Great, thanks Dr. Smith."

So for the next eight or nine months, that's exactly what she did. I heard from her every day except the days that I had an appointment with her. At this point in therapy I was seeing her twice a week, on Mondays and Fridays. When my insurance ran out, she saw me anyway. She was that committed to helping me.

I could not wait to see her and each time I left her office the pain was so great that I would relapse. The only thing that kept me going was knowing I would hear from her soon. I was at a loss to understand why I formed such a deep attachment with Ann and Dr. Smith. I knew one thing for sure—I must break it off.

Chapter Twenty-Six
THE END COMMENCES

The end of my relationship with Dr. Smith came slowly. Actually I did not even see it coming until it was too late. It began as I waited in her waiting room. An unattractive, almost masculine-looking woman came out of Dr. Smith's office. She had an unlit cigarette dangling from her lips. Following her closely was Dr. Smith. The woman looked straight ahead and did not look at me. I thought to myself, *What a pig.* Dr. Smith nodded to me and said, "Come on in." I followed her into her office and sat down. I watched Dr. Smith, as I always did, but this time she acted differently. She locked her office door. I thought to myself, *Hmm, that's strange, why would she do that?* I swiveled my chair and looked out the big picture window, as I had done many times before. The unattractive woman was sitting on the office porch, smoking her cigarette.

Dr. Smith and I began talking, mostly small talk, and every so often I would look out to see if the woman had left. It made me uncomfortable to know she was there. I asked Dr. Smith, "Why did you lock the door?"

She said matter-of-factly, "On your way out a woman may tell you she wants to fuck you."

I jerked back in shock. She explained that I should be aware of what this woman might say to me.

"I cannot talk about her case, but she suffers from multiple personalities and right now, Ellie, she is in the personality that cannot drive, and she may ask you to take her home."

Dr. Smith went on to say that the personality she is in now believes that the only way to get home is if she lets me have sex with her.

I told Dr. Smith that I could take care of myself if the woman accosted me. In truth, I was sickened and embarrassed by the thought that this creature might come on to me. Dr. Smith's office was the one place where safety reigned and I would not have to deal with the filth and sludge that I had to endure as a child. With the snap of a finger, a lock of a door, my safety was compromised. I felt alone once again.

After my session, I cautiously walked out to the porch. Dr. Smith was right behind me. She walked me to my car. I turned to her and said, "Are you going to be all right? What if the woman goes into a homicidal personality?" "I'll be all right," she said.

I was frightened for her. When I arrived at home I called her, "Are you OK?" "Yes, she left."

I thought to myself, *I do not need this shit of worrying about someone else—I cannot take care of myself—I* certainly did not have the energy to worry about Dr. Smith. Dr. Smith took nearly every precaution to make sure my path did not cross again with that strange woman. Well, almost.

As Dr. Smith was making preparations for her annual month-long trip to Florida, she assured me that she would come back for a week during that month to see some of her patients, including me. She also told me what days she would be flying in and back out. She said, "I made you the last appointment, and I'll be leaving for the airport after your session."

After gathering up some courage, I offered to drive her to the airport. I was leery because I knew that I might be overstepping boundaries with her, especially after the whipping Ann gave me about boundaries. The positive part was that I began to feel more comfortable and able to express myself with Dr. Smith. With that freedom, I stepped out and risked rejection.

Dr. Smith said, "I do have a ride, but thanks anyway."

"Did you decide against me because of the patient-therapist relationship."

"No, someone had offered to drive me to the airport before your offer."

That made me feel better.

Toward the end of my session, before Dr. Smith was to fly back to Florida, I glanced out the window, and there on Dr. Smith's porch sat the unattractive woman. I turned slowly toward Dr. Smith and said, "Is she taking you to the airport?"

"Yes."

"Of all the people in the world, why her?"

"Because she picked me up at my house this morning, and since I do not have my car here, she offered to drive me to the airport."

"Why couldn't you have told her to pick you up after my session ended?"

"I thought you would be gone by the time she arrived."

Livid, I walked out.

I was well aware I did not like this woman, but I did not understand why I had so much contempt for her. To know that Dr. Smith chose her over me was brutally painful. Like a dejected child, I was jealous over the attention this woman was getting. However, it was confusing because I had seen Dr. Smith give another patient some TLC and it did not bother me. As a matter of fact, this particular patient would spend all day, many days, in Dr. Smith's waiting room. She would pack her lunch and just sit there all day. Sometimes when I came in for my sessions she would be sitting there, and we would talk. She seemed like a nice young lady, and, of course, I do not know what her problem was, but I certainly could appreciate it if she had an attachment to Dr. Smith because if I could have, I would have done the same thing.

Meanwhile, I continued to be puzzled as to why this unattractive woman could prime my emotion until immense anger and hatred for her spewed out.

The Gift of Hurt

Then, one lonely night while Dr. Smith was in Florida, just after I finished my second drink, everything came together. The masculine-looking woman who wanted to fuck me for a ride home from Dr. Smith's office looked just like the person who accosted me in the bathroom of the rat-trapped theater when I was a child. I knew one thing for sure and that was that I could not feel comfortable in Dr. Smith's office again. I perceived her as sleeping with the enemy. Now I had to deal with Dr. Smith being pals with what I viewed as a sexual abuser. If the woman wanted to fuck me while she was in one of her personalities, what was to keep her from molesting a child—a child like I was?

While wallowing in my betrayed-by-Dr.-Smith mode, I remembered that she often commented on my talent for writing. She seemed to enjoy reading my work. With that in mind, coupled with my irrational thoughts, I took the journal I had written in for over ten-years and cut it up into what seemed like millions of pieces. I gathered all the pieces and mailed them to her while she vacationed in Florida. That action left her completely dumbfounded.

Chapter Twenty-Seven
A TALENT DISCOVERED

I not only had to struggle with the pain of Ann and the perceived betrayal by Dr. Smith, I had to struggle to maintain my sanity at my job. I was expected to type exams and correspondence and handle any work the professors asked me to do. However, I was growing weary and bored, and I yearned for new digs. With the endorsement from Dr. Smith as well as my mentor, Professor Wilcoxin, that I had a talent for expressing myself with the written word, I decided to concentrate on something that I enjoyed—writing. Before the debacle with the unattractive woman, Dr. Smith suggested that writing to her what I could not speak about during therapy might be helpful. She said, "Maybe if you become famous, Ann will talk to you." Whoa! That was all I needed to hear. Famous plus journalist equals Ann speaking to me.

In my desire to become a published writer, detailing my premature termination with Ann might prove to be interesting to a specialized magazine—and it was. A professional paper in the mental health field printed my piece. I sent a copy to Ann, hoping she would respond. She returned the copy to Dr. Smith. To my knowledge, Ann has never read the article.

My mind kept swimming with ways to become famous and do what no neophyte had done before. I thought, *I'll write Supreme Court Justice Sandra Day O'Connor, First Lady Hillary Clinton, Attorney General Janet Reno, and my Congresswoman, Marcy Kaptur, to see if they would allow me to interview them—for my senior thesis.* Then I would send out the interviews to magazines and when they were published, voila! I would be good enough for Ann—she would see some worth in me.

Unfortunately, Mrs. Clinton's deputy press secretary wrote that the First Lady had too many commitments. Reno's office called saying that the timing was bad because of the problems they were having with a militia group. However, Justice O'Connor and Congresswoman Kaptur agreed. I was to meet O'Connor at 10:30 in the morning in mid 1990, and later that afternoon I would meet with Kaptur. After these women agreed to be interviewed, I began to get nervous.

I was given the opportunity to meet with Justice O'Connor because she had met me in 1991 when she visited my town to judge a moot court competition at a local law college. She offered to have the interview conducted over the phone, but I wanted the interview to take place in her chambers in Washington, D.C. She agreed.

I began to feel a sense of confidence after these distinguished women agreed to be interviewed. I was preoccupied with the trip to D.C. when the bottom suddenly fell out. I received a horrible phone call from the hospital in late winter in the mid 1990s informing me that my youngest son, Rick, had been injured in an automobile accident. The woman said, "Please come to the hospital as soon as possible."

"Is he alive?"

"He is confused."

"We're on our way."

I wrote the following article, which appeared in the local paper. It chronicles Rick's injury:

The Call That All Parents Fear

I shall always remember receiving the phone call that all parents fear.

It was Saturday evening and the roads were glazed with snow as my husband and I rushed to the hospital, not knowing if we would arrive in time to see our son alive. The call came from the hospital informing me that my son Rick had been injured in an automobile accident. I was told to come to the hospital emergency room as soon as possible and to please drive safely. The first question I asked the woman on the phone was "Is he alive?" She said, "He is confused." I asked no more questions.

When we arrived, we were immediately ushered into the trauma room to witness the trauma team working on our son. He was unconscious from a head injury. As I held his hand the doctor explained to us what they were doing and what to expect in the next few days.

We were asked to leave the room and meet them in the Surgical Intensive Care Unit (SICU), where they would give us an update on his condition. Like robots in a science fiction movie, we obeyed. Before I left, I bent over to kiss Rick, but I could find nowhere on his beautiful face that was free of blood from his head wound. I kissed his cheek and remember thinking, *My boy is in trouble.*

As my husband and I left the room I asked the doctor, "Is my son going to die?" He replied, "Your son is in serious condition, but I believe he will live." The relief that swept over us was short-lived as we were informed that with a head wound as serious as our son had sustained, major complications requiring surgery may occur.

The SICU waiting room was filled with strangers of all shapes, sizes, ages, and colors. The scent of freshly brewed coffee was a pleasant reminder of happier times. The television was turned on, but people paid no attention to it. It seemed like it was there as a symbol of the normality we all had lost.

Still in shock and filled with fear, we were comforted and gave comfort to our other children as they joined the vigil for their brother.

I clearly recall the feeling of despair I felt when I saw my son and all the tubes that were connected to him after he was placed in the SICU. When I left his room and stepped through the doors into the hallway, I began to cry. I walked toward the waiting room and saw my other children standing outside the doorway.

For some reason, I asked for a piece of gum. It was at that moment a woman overheard our conversation and offered me a piece of gum. She said, "Everything will be okay." She also hugged me. I thanked her and retreated to the small area of the waiting room that our family had commandeered.

As we started to acclimate ourselves to hospital living, a young woman who was also keeping vigil for a family member approached us and shared some of the ins and outs of the waiting room. She showed us where the coffee, tea, and hot chocolate were kept. Where we could find crackers and cookies, and how to secure blankets and pillows for some sleeping in the long hours ahead. It was then I began to witness the unusual bonding that takes place between people who share a common emotion—the fear of losing a loved one.

Another example of the kindness people showed one another was when I was sitting and pondering Rick's fate. A young woman sat beside me and asked how my son was doing. I told her my story, and she told me hers. Sadly, her husband had been involved in an accident at an auto plant. While we were talking, the kind woman who hugged me and gave me a piece of gum sat down with us. She was the victim's mother.

The hours turned into days. Each visit with Rick renewed my belief that if he did regain consciousness we may still have lost him mentally. We were counseled on the mental and physical damage a head wound of this magnitude could cause, and that warning was realized the first time I talked with him when he regained consciousness.

I asked him if he knew where he was. He did not. I asked him who I was, and he said faintly, "You're my teacher." I was devastated. I wanted to cry, alone, but there was not a private place that I could retreat. Another kind lady whose family member was in the SICU directed me to a room where I could be alone. I used that room several more times over the course of Rick's hospital stay.

Each day would bring renewed hope that Rick would regain his memory. Then, just when we would become excited because his vitals were good and the tubes were starting to be removed, there would be a backslide and they would have to insert new tubes. It seemed at those times the people in the waiting room would come through with little words of support and cheer, like, "I saw your son Rick and he looked good. He is a very handsome young man." I needed to hear that, and it was from the man whose mother was recuperating from heart surgery. I found myself giving support and comfort to them as well as I asked how their loved ones were doing.

The Gift of Hurt

We are most fortunate that our story has a happy ending. Too often when parents receive that phone call from the hospital, it is a precursor to a notification of a fatality.

Rick hopes to attend the local university this fall. He seems fully recovered physically, although he did not walk away unscathed. He does suffer from a slight personality change and sometimes has difficulty coordinating his thoughts with his words. The personality change will always be a remnant of the head wound he suffered in the accident. However, our family believes that it is a small price to pay for Rick's life.

Chapter Twenty-Eight
AN ALMOST DEADLY REVELATION

While waiting for word about Rick, I telephoned Dr. Smith from the hospital emergency room in a panic. It was comforting to speak with her. Though I did not verbalize it to her, I wanted her to come up to the hospital for support. I sat in the waiting room, closed my eyes, bowed my head, and pretended that she was sitting next to me. When she did not show up, and when I realized she was not coming, I vowed to continue to fight my attachment to her even to the extent of planning another suicide attempt.

Also, I continued to have a difficult time forgiving Dr. Smith for treating the unattractive woman, who mirrored the person who accosted me in the theater bathroom decades earlier, in a preferential manner. The situation became so disturbing that I could not enter her office because that horrid woman had contaminated it.

After exchanging some not-so-nice words with Dr. Smith, she agreed to meet me anywhere I wanted. I chose a local restaurant down the street from her office. I asked Grace to join me beforehand for dinner. At that time Dr. Smith and Grace met. When Dr. Smith arrived, Grace bid us goodbye and left. Things really became quite ugly and unprofessional between Dr. Smith and me. I kept badgering her about the unattractive woman who wanted to fuck me and even started to spew platitudes about her knowledge of psychology. She became angry with me and said, "I'm going to leave if you keep baiting me."

"I'm not baiting you."

I smarted off again, and she left. A few days later we talked, and I agreed to try to resume therapy in her office.

My excessive drinking was causing difficulty for everyone, mainly because of the personality change it caused in me. I was impatient and a belligerent bitch. Dr. Smith continued to harp on me about my drinking. In what I viewed as a moment of weakness, I told her I would try to quit drinking, mainly for her. She said, "I don't care what reason you use as long as you quit." She encouraged me to try an antidepressant too. I bolted like a bucking bronco at that suggestion.

It was an impossibly difficult time in my life, but Dr. Smith and my family were there to support me every step of the way. I was experiencing the usual alcohol withdrawal symptoms of craving, headaches, and nervousness. I guess on the big scale I fared better than a lot of people. One evening Dr. Smith called just to see how I was doing. She asked, "Is there anything I can do to help you?"

"No—I don't know if I can do this."

"You can do it, Ellie."

I tried for a while longer but I could not do it. I started drinking again.

After considerable pressure I succumbed to everybody's' advice and asked my doctor to prescribe an antidepressant. I reluctantly picked up a month's supply at the pharmacy and started to drive—nowhere in particular, I just drove. I saw the pills on the seat next to me and in a fit of anger and disappointment with myself opened the container and threw them out the window. They bounced around like jumping beans on the hot asphalt. I told Dr. Smith what I did, and she said, frustrated, "The pills are expensive and some of my patients would love to be able to afford them—and you threw them out."

After being censured by Dr. Smith, I agreed to try it again. This time when I picked up the 30 pills at the pharmacy, I would use them to stage my suicide. I began a plan to stockpile the pills and end my suffering.

I had already made plans to visit my friend Kathy again in British Columbia. The trip was to take place in three months. I concocted a scheme to ingest the ninety pills after my visit with her. I had a room reserved in Seattle, would be alone, and thought it would be the perfect time to take the pills.

Dr. Smith, in her caring way, had arranged a session for me the day before I was scheduled to fly out. The session was uneventful, and I left as usual—with the unbearable pain caused by the separation from her. About a mile down the road I had the overwhelming desire to say a final goodbye to her. I quickly turned my car around and went back to her office. Just as I pulled into the parking lot, I saw her walking toward her car. I drove up next to it, got out and walked up to her, and hugged her. I am sure I shocked the hell out of her because one of my problems was that I did not like anyone touching me. She asked for another hug, and I gave her one.

At that moment she probably thought that she had finally made some great leap in therapy, that some mammoth breakthrough had occurred. What I had done was finalize our relationship. Saying goodbye to my family was also done in a final way.

I even went so far as to go through each of my dresser drawers and fold and straighten each piece of clothing and lingerie. That way people would think I was tidy. I sent my attorney a letter that was to be opened only in the event of my death. In that envelope was a statement ordering my family not to start any litigation against Ann. I blamed myself.

I proceeded on my journey. I had a wonderful visit with Kathy, and when I left her it was again very sad. While I was with her, I thought maybe I would not kill myself. Maybe I was making a mistake.

I drove the long way from British Columbia to Seattle and checked into my room. I was alone, and very vulnerable. My incessant drinking intensified my state of confusion and pain. It was a pain I was certain no one understood or could remedy and one that I was sure they were tired of seeing and hearing.

The first thing I did was hit the ice machine so I could fix myself a drink. I spilled the pills on the table in my room. I counted them and came up with ninety pills. I turned the TV on, threw a couple more cubes in my drink, and sat on the bed looking at the pills and the TV, then the pills, TV, and finally the pills. I thought about Dr. Smith, Ann, and my family. I did not want to hurt anyone—that was not my intention. I did not want to go down as Dr. Smith's failure and make her feel badly. In a coherent moment, I called Dr. Smith. She was there.

We talked mostly small talk and just before I hung up I said, "I've got ninety pills in front of me."

I cannot tell you what she said to me next. I draw a blank about that time. What I do remember is that she told me to call her back at 3:45 p.m. She said she had to leave for a while and would be back by then. She warned me, "If I do not hear from you I'll call your husband."

"OK, OK, I'll call you then."

Knowing that I could call her and that I was not alone was enough to help me hang on.

To play it safe, after I hung up, I left my room and walked to the top of the hill that overlooked the hotel. I thought that Dr. Smith might have called the police. I waited a good hour or so and returned to my room, confident that this could be handled between Dr. Smith and me.

I decided to wait until 4 p.m. instead of 3:45 in case Dr. Smith was not home. I wanted to be sure she would not miss my call. About 3:50 my phone rang, and when I answered I heard Matt's voice. He said, "Dr. Smith called me when you did not call her back at 3:45. Why are you doing this?"

"I can't take the pain anymore, Matt."

We talked for a long time, and all the while I was playing with the pills—lining them up like a ninety-car train. Before I hung up, I promised to hold off from taking the pills. When I flew into Detroit, Matt was there. He asked, "Are you okay?"

"No, Matt I need Ann and Dr. Smith."

Dr. Smith asked if I would like to go in the hospital. I defiantly said, "No."

"I will not see you again, Ellie, unless you turn the pills over to me or someone, anyone." She voiced that she was not going to treat someone who had such little regard for her own life. I think, in essence, I told her to go to hell. Eventually, I did come around and agreed to give up the pills to Grace.

I also decided to work harder at therapy and take antidepressants, one at a time. My drinking still posed a problem as I was unwilling to stop. While reading the newspaper one day, I came across an article in our local paper relating a story about problem drinkers. The article said that sometimes if problem drinkers limit themselves to one or two drinks a day it would bring about the same outcome as going cold turkey. In a last-ditch effort to gain control over my abusive drinking, I followed the suggestion of that article and imposed a limit on myself. To my surprise it worked for me! Although I slipped on occasion, for the most part I had successfully brought my drinking under control.

Although the pills seemed to uplift my spirits and my general outlook on life, they did not minimize the pain every time I left Dr. Smith. I still felt lost and alone. About two-months later I decided that I did not want to take the pills any longer. I took myself off them and waited to see the results. I did not notice a difference.

A few weeks later, in a moment of strength (where it came from I do not know), I decided to terminate therapy with Dr. Smith.

"Ellie, I don't think it is a good idea."

"I didn't think you would encourage it, Dr. Smith. But you're killing me."

Though she was adamantly against it, unlike Ann, she allowed me closure.

We met on her office porch, and I tried to explain why I could not continue with therapy. She listened, but I know that she thought I was making a horrific mistake. I told her that I was grateful for all her help, but terminating therapy was the best thing for both of us. I went on to explain that I caused her a lot of worry and that she was under enough personal stress and did not need more from me. I also reiterated that, "Your nurturing is killing me, and I am weary of hurting every time I leave you." Though I wore sunglasses so Dr. Smith could not see the tears that rolled down my cheeks, it was difficult to mask the choking lump in my throat and my breaking heart. She wished me the best and nonchalantly returned to her office. I returned to my car and drove off hurting but relieved. I cried at my loss, but it was comforting to know that I could, at least, talk with her again—so I thought.

Chapter Twenty-Nine
DÉJÀ-VU

A couple of days after I terminated therapy with Dr. Smith, Matt told me he had lost his job—again. I immediately poured myself a drink, and then another and another. I hated the man who fired my husband. Unfortunately, my brother, Paul, owned the company he worked for at the time. I blamed my brother for Matt's termination, too. In a drunken rage I called Paul, but his voicemail clicked on. I proceeded to say horrible things on it. He called back, but I would not talk with him—I was still very angry.

I tried to deal with Matt's job loss and my belief that it was my brother's fault—but I just could not cope. I called Dr. Smith and asked her to take me back. She said, "I'll take you back but it will have to be under new conditions."

"I understand."

A day or so later I received a letter from her in which she stated in no uncertain terms that she would not take me back and would not allow me any contact with her. She also said she did not want my family contacting her. Wow, déjà-vu—another therapist bites the dust. I said to myself, *Ellie, you have the uncanny knack of going through therapists like some women go through pantyhose.*

I thought I was going to die from the pain of Dr. Smith's rejection. I started to panic because I thought I could not live without her.

"Oh dear God, what do I do? I cannot make it without Dr. Smith."

I even conjured up the thought of suicide again.

It confused me so, because these women, these therapists, gave me home phone numbers, asked me to call them by first names, allowed me to know personal problems, and in a millisecond, turned it off and became formal, contradictory, and cruel. It further confused me when they placed so much importance on intimacy and the value of human relationships and yet could turn everything on and off like a light switch.

Chapter Thirty
THE AWAKENING

A week or so after Dr. Smith's rejection letter, I still struggled with the consequences of being alone without a therapist. I was vulnerable, had no where to turn, and lived in a state of panic. The feeling was akin to falling on your back and not being able to catch your breath.

What happened next I can only call an awakening, an epiphany if you will. This epiphany occurred while I was brushing my teeth one morning. I looked closely into the bathroom mirror and this is what I saw: a weak, Godless, selfish, angry, and useless woman. A woman who had caused pain and worry to the people who loved and cared about her. I cannot give a definitive answer or cause about what prompted this truly miraculous about-face. However, I can offer an uneducated theory as to what worked for me.

First, I knew I could control my drinking. Second, if I could control my drinking, I could do anything. Third, I believed that Dr. Smith's rejection was her way of saying, "I like you Ellie and you can make it through anything and gain complete control of your life." Writing that rejection letter had to be difficult. We both knew if she took me back as her patient I would only continue to be dependent on her, which would lead to my death. Fourth, I began adopting Dr. Smith's philosophy into my everyday relationships. Her philosophy simply states that, "the joy of living, connecting and developing emotional intimacy with people is or can be a part of living." Fifth, the undying devotion and love of my husband, children, extended family and friends helped me. Sixth, though I scorned them at the time, the antidepressants helped give me a jump-start with coping. Last, and with reverent respect and faith, I believe my recovery was precipitated by my awakening faith in a higher power, one not of this world.

After my half-decade pity party came to an end, I found myself actually happy when I awoke in the morning. I anticipated the day. I started to enjoy the little things in life, like having a cup of coffee with Matt on our patio. I enjoyed swimming and barbecue cookouts with my family in our back yard. I went fishing and boating. When I walked or ran, it was for fun and my cardiovascular system. I found myself excited at what life had in store for me. I was pleased because I could control my anger. I knew my anger was still there and I would have to keep it in check for the rest of my life, but considering all that had happened to me, that was not an unreasonable commitment.

I found myself singing and dancing to music while I curled my hair in the morning. I was like a child on Christmas morning in that I opened up the present that I had wished for. I was reborn, and within that painful birthing process I had conquered, but more importantly survived, one of the worst debilitating demons that stalks humankind—mental illness.

I called my Uncle Robert and Aunt Joanne. I had not talked with them since we became estranged twenty-five-years earlier after my father's death. We never discussed why we drifted apart, and actually it did not seem important any longer. It just felt good to see them and to include them in my life again.

I began spending more time with my family, friends, and the loves of my life, my grandsons, Zachary and Blake. I opened myself up to my loved ones as never before. One case in point is my former professor, Esther Wilcoxin. As a teacher, she helped me achieve much more than I thought possible. I not only excelled in my schoolwork but also became a published writer, received a press club award and a nomination for employee of the year, and graduated magna cum laude. Esther started out as my professor, became my mentor, most ardent supporter, and, I am proud to say, my friend.

While planning another solo vacation trip to visit Kathy, I took the liberty of calling Esther and asked if I could take her up on her previous invitation to visit with her and her husband, Jim, in Utah. They were truly happy about my visit to their summer condo and anxiously awaited my arrival at the Salt Lake City Airport.

After helping me settle into their guestroom, they showed me around town. For the next couple of days I was treated like royalty. Every so often I would think of Dr. Smith and how pleased she would be that I was finally coming into my own. I wished I could talk with her and tell her how neat Utah was, but I knew I could not. As far as Ann was concerned, I did think of her, too. Only I thought, *fuck you, Ann!*

After Jim and Esther saw me off at the Salt Lake City Airport, I was on my way to Seattle, where I rented a car and drove to British Columbia, to spend five days with Kathy. It was glorious seeing her again. We always have a good time together, and it gave me a chance to relax and count my blessings by the beautiful Okanagan Lake. When I left to head back to Seattle, it broke my heart. But I was confident that I would see Kathy again. When I arrived in Seattle, I enjoyed my last night of vacation, all alone, in my hotel room and never entertained thoughts of destroying myself. It was quite a contrast to the previous year when I made a train of destruction out of the ninety stockpiled pills.

Upon my arrival at my home airport, Matt was waiting for me. We kissed and he said, "I really missed you."

"I missed you too Matt."

We gabbed and laughed all the way home from the airport. Since my brush with death, we have become closer than I ever thought possible. We have learned to trust and share our deepest hurts, worries, loves, and passions. Our marriage has truly evolved into what holy matrimony should be. Our relationship has also evolved into a phenomenal coupling in that we are no longer afraid to trust and to share.

I now trust and can reach out to my wonderful sister-in-law Grace, who endured much of my emotional turmoil and helped me with her unconditional love, patience, and time. Along with that I made a concerted effort to reach out and cultivate friendships with students in my undergraduate classes as well as some of the professors that taught me.

When I graduated, six months after terminating therapy with Dr. Smith, I experienced one of the most thrilling moments of my life. It was an accomplishment that I had worked long and hard to achieve. To add a couple of cherries to the already delicious sundae was the moment, before receiving a handshake and scroll from the dean of my college, that Esther walked over and said she wanted to hug me before I was an official graduate. As I returned to my seat, I had to pass the area where the graduates and faculty of the college in which I worked were seated. When I walked by, they all stood up, students and faculty alike, to cheer and applaud me. I went over and hugged many of them before returning to my seat. It was a wonderful, memorable morning.

As I continued my journey to regain mental health and while sorting out my feelings for Dr. Smith and Ann, I read a disturbing article in the local newspaper. Ann's husband had been arrested for sexually abusing and penetrating two nine-year-old girls. He was being held without bond at a local jail. If convicted, he would likely spend the rest of his life in prison.

When I saw the headline, I jumped up from my chair in shock. I just stood there, clutching the paper, with my first thought being of Ann's pain. My next thought was how ironic it was that Ann loved and married a man like the one who abused me when I was nine-years-old. Did she know her husband was a pervert, a pedophile? A man does not just suddenly become a pedophile one day. It was upsetting and difficult for me to comprehend that at the time Ann was treating me and trying to make some sense to me about my childhood sexual abuses that her own husband was probably out there victimizing children.

I showed the article to my family. They felt that there was some sort of justice that had been dished out to Ann since she caused me such hurt and her rejection almost caused my death. I felt then as I do now—I will always have a deep affection for Ann and my heart went out to her—that plain, that simple. I gained nothing from her pain—my love does not work that way.

I was distressed at the newspaper article and called Dr. Smith. Her voicemail picked up. I left a message telling her about the article and saying that I did not want therapy, I just wanted to talk with her about this revelation. She never responded to my request. She treated me as though I had fallen off the face of the earth.

I often wondered how I would react if I ever ran into Dr. Smith or Ann in public. An accidental meeting would be my final test. Would I run up crying and drop to my knees, begging, "Please Ann, please Dr. Smith forgive me. Please like me again. Please accept me again."

Perhaps I would run up and spit in their faces and exclaim, "To hell with you Ann. To hell with you Dr. Smith. How dare you dismiss me. How dare you cause me harm."

The question was, would I ever see them again?

A week or so after Ann's husband's arrest I was finishing my usual daily walk in the park on a bright Sunday morning. It was the same park at which I asked Ann to meet me those many years ago. While I was returning to my car, walking toward me was a woman with a dog. There was a young man with her. We kept walking toward each other and I thought to myself, *There you go again thinking you see Ann.* Only this time it really was her. My mouth dropped open, and my heart started to race. As we approached each other, I could see the panic in her face. It was like she was a trapped rat. She first looked down, but then looked up, probably to see if her life was in danger and to see if I had pulled a weapon of some sort. As I passed her I said, "Hi Ann, how are you?" I heard some sound, mumbling, maybe even a groan from her, but for the life of me I could not make it out. My question about how I would react if I ever saw her was finally answered. I just kept walking. I have to admit that I did turn and look back at her with tears in my eyes while I embraced a very special gift that Ann gave me—the gift of hurt.

When I got to my car, I fell apart. I cried and was in pain. But I did it—I saw her and I did not crumble. I was able to regain some of the dignity I had lost years before. It took a few days, but I recovered from our chance meeting at the park. It was my belief that the young man with her was her son, the same boy, I believe, who called and left those horrible slurs on my voicemail many years ago. Being that it was only a week or so after her husband's arrest, she was probably trying to explain to him why his father was a pedophile. Ann's husband ultimately pleaded guilty to child abuse and is now spending eight to thirty years in prison. The paper said that the judge even recommended that he not be eligible for early release.

In another strange turn of events, I ran into Dr. Smith about a year after our last session. I had just finished having lunch with Esther and looked up and saw Dr. Smith taking her seat a couple of tables away from us.

Esther saw my face and thought there had been an accident outside. When I told her what had prompted my startled look, she said, "Come on let's get out of here."

"Esther, I want to say hello to Dr. Smith."

While she paid the bill, I went over to Dr. Smith's table and tapped her on the shoulder. I put my hand out, hoping she would shake it. She shook my hand as I asked, "How are you doing?" She seemed surprised and exuded a rather aloof attitude. Hopefully she reacted that way because I caught her off guard and not because the sight of me repelled her.

Chapter Thirty-One
EPILOGUE

It took me years to realize how much pain my inappropriate behavior caused everyone. My relationship with Ann and Dr. Smith could have turned out so differently had I not acted irrationally and impulsively. It could have ended on a positive note had my panic not exacerbated the situation.

What I experienced in that dark abyss of mental illness I pray never to experience again. I have gained a new understanding and compassion for people who suffer from any form of mental illness and/or disorders. I hope my experience will go far to help the general population understand how critical it is that the mentally ill receive help and support.

Ann once told me that "Good people do bad things." It is with that saying that maybe we can try to reach out to help the good people who suffer from the sickness of mental illness and forgive them for the bad things they do. Above all else, we must treat them with patience and kindness.

It has been years since Ann talked with me. It has been years since Dr. Smith forbade me to contact her. More than likely, I shall go to my death hurting whenever I think of these women. More than likely, I will always remember the pedophile who violated me in the park. More than likely, I shall recall the early and sad deaths of my parents. And, more than likely, I will go to my death remembering all the abuses I suffered while growing up. But, more importantly, I will always embrace the love my family and friends showed me during the lowest ebb of my life. The paradox of not only my life but of many lives is that without living with the gift of hurt we would never have experienced the profound meaning of intimacy and connecting with one another.

About The Author

Pamela Crabtree is a nationally published author living in Holland, OH. Pam has been married to Fred since 1966. That union produced four children, Patrick, Amy (Robert) Gibson, Tod and Eric. They are also the grandparents of Zachary and Blake Gibson.

Pam is currently studying for her Masters degree at The University of Toledo. "The Gift of Hurt" is her first book and she is uniquely qualified to have written it since she has lived every moment of it.